5 STEPS TO A 5

Writing the AP English Essay
2018

Barbara L. Murphy
Estelle M. Rankin

Mc Graw Hill Education

New York Chicago San Francisco Athens London Madrid
Mexico City Milan New Delhi Singapore Sydney Toronto

1 2 3 4 5 6 7 8 9   LHS   22 21 20 19 18 17

ISBN   978-1-259-86310-3
MHID   1-259-86310-7

e-ISBN   978-1-259-86311-0
e-MHID   1-259-86311-5

Trademarks: McGraw-Hill Education, the McGraw-Hill Education logo, *5 Steps to a 5*, and related trade dress are trademarks or registered trademarks of the McGraw-Hill Education and/or its affiliates in the United States and other countries and may not be used without written permission. All other trademarks are the property of their respective owners. McGraw-Hill Education is not associated with any product or vendor mentioned in this book.

AP, Advanced Placement Program, and College Board are registered trademarks of the College Board, which was not involved in the production of, and does not endorse, this product.

The series editor was Grace Freedson, and the project editor was Del Franz.
Series design by Jane Tenenbaum.

McGraw-Hill Education products are available at special quantity discounts to use as premiums and sales or for use in corporate training programs. To contact a representative, please visit the Contact Us pages at www.mhprofessional.com.

CONTENTS

5 Steps to a 5, Writing the AP English Essay is meant to be a supplement to both the AP English Language and Composition and the AP English Literature and Composition courses. There is no way to take the place of the instruction, interaction, feedback, and growth that takes place in the English classroom. What we hope to accomplish in this text is similar to what a personal trainer can do in the gym: provide those eager and willing to learn with information and activities designed to increase writing endurance and to enhance, fine tune, and shape the writing muscles being used in the AP English classroom.

Although specifically designed for the AP English student, the concepts, strategies, techniques, and skills examined in this book can easily be applied to college-level writing assignments across the curriculum.

ACKNOWLEDGMENTS

Our love and appreciation to Leah and Allan for their constant support and encouragement. Our very special thanks to the many English instructors and English students who were so gracious and cooperative in granting us access to their expertise and their writing. We particularly would like to acknowledge the following educators: Diane Antonucci, Joyce Bisso, Mrs. Curran, Sandi Forsythe, Scott Honig, Barbara Inners, Mike Kramer, Margaret Rice, Joan Rosenberg, Ed Schmieder, Joanne Seale, Conni Shelnut, Doris Valliante, Rosemary Varade, Karl Zemer, and Pat Zippel.

The following students were willing to be risk takers in allowing their writings to be incorporated into the pages of this book. They, and all of our students, are the primary reason why all of us do the work we do.

Matthew Bergman
Kate Boicourt
Jaime Burke
Alyssa Dunn
Jessica Fisher
Allison Ivans
Adam Katz
Karin Katz
Adam Kaufman
Josh Kazdin
Brian Kelly
Michael Kleinman
Daniel Lange
Tamara Lee
Michelle Rinke
Sally Robley

Dana Schenendorf
Carly Seidman
Jamelle Sing
Matthew Singer
Lenny Slutsky
Limor Spector
Alex Stein
Matthew Stoff
Lindsey Thalheim
Michael Tolkin
Danielle Tumminio
Deborah Wassel
Diana Watral
Amanda Weingarten
Zachary Zwillinger

ABOUT THE AUTHORS

Barbara Murphy taught AP Language and other college-level courses at Jericho High School for over 20 years. She has been a reader of the AP Language and Composition exam since 1993 and is a consultant for the College Board's AP Language and Composition and its Building for Success divisions, for whom she has conducted workshops, conferences, specialty conference presentations, and Summer Institutes. Barbara is currently on the faculty of Syracuse University's Project Advance in English. After earning her BA from Duquesne University and her MA from the University of Pittsburgh, Ms. Murphy did her doctoral course work at Columbia University. She also holds professional certifications in still photography and motion picture production and is one of the founding members of the women's film company, Ishtar Films.

Estelle Rankin taught AP Literature at Jericho High School for over 25 years. She was honored with the AP Literature Teacher of the Year award by the College Board in 1996. Estelle also received the Long Island Teacher of the Year award in 1990. She was also the recipient of the Cornell University Presidential Scholars' award and has been recognized by the C. W. Post Master Teachers Program.

Ms. Rankin earned her BA from Adelphi University and her MA from Hofstra University. She has pursued further graduate work in the field of creative studies at Queens College and Brooklyn College.

Estelle has done extensive work in the research and development of film, drama, and creative writing curricula, and has participated in numerous AP Literature conferences and workshops, is a consultant for Building Success, and is also a Literature presenter for the Advanced Placement Specialty conferences. In addition, she pioneered a "senior initiative mentoring program" based on internships and service, and has conducted many English workshops for both teachers and students at high schools and middle schools for New York's Board of Cooperative Educational Services (BOCES). Her first teachers were her parents, Edward and Selma Stern.

Ms. Rankin and Ms. Murphy are also the coauthors of McGraw-Hill Education's *5 Steps to a 5: AP English Language*, *AP English Literature*, and *Writing an Outstanding College Application Essay*.

Set Up Your Study Program

CHAPTER 1

Introduction to the Training Program

IN THIS CHAPTER

Summary: Find the answers to your questions about the AP English essays

Key Ideas
- ✪ Discover what constitutes an AP English essay
- ✪ Examine different essay requirements for AP English Language and AP English Literature
- ✪ Explore a generic set of AP English essay rubrics

Meet Your Trainers

"The task of a writer consists in being able to make something out of an idea."
—Thomas Mann

Welcome to our writing training program. Obviously, if you've decided to purchase and read this book, you already have an interest in writing. Good for you. Now, take a moment to clarify for yourself why you feel the need for training. (Check those that apply.) Perhaps:

_____ You want to do well in your AP English class.
_____ You freeze when writing timed essays.
_____ You have trouble finding the right things to say.
_____ You don't like to write exam essays.
_____ You can't finish an exam essay on time.
_____ You frequently have writer's block.

You might also have chosen this text because you're interested in or unsure about one or more of the following aspects of the writing process. (Check those that apply.)

_____ pointers
_____ planning
_____ models
_____ exercises
_____ standards
_____ evaluation

We're betting that you checked off more than one of these items. With this in mind, we're going to help you address each of these areas of concern about writing. Think of us as your AP Writing personal trainers. You have the ability, and you certainly have the desire and will. Together, we will develop and strengthen those writing muscles you need to compose effective AP English essays.

It is important to understand that the purpose of this training is to help you to develop as an AP writer throughout the year, NOT just for performance on a single exam at the end of the term. But, obviously, if you train with a specific goal in mind, your performance on the exam should be enhanced.

Having said that, there are probably many questions that you would like to ask about AP English essays. Here are a few that students have asked over the years.

Questions and Answers About the AP English Essay

What's the Difference Between the "Average High School English Essay" and One Termed an "Advanced Placement English Essay?"

You can begin to answer this question yourself just by deciding which of the following is an average high school essay and which is an AP English essay.

A

Verbal prowess has certainly played a great role in history. An individual's language is instrumental in the formation of his personal identity just as the language of a given culture plays a large part in the formation of its communal identity. Language can be a key to success in both personal and public causes. Back in the early 1800s, a young black slave Phyllis Wheatley set herself apart through poetry and led her readers to a fuller awareness of the plight of slaves in the United States. In the later 1800s, a very eloquent ex-slave Frederick Douglass spoke on behalf of his race, expertly manipulating his words into an extremely effective weapon. Douglass's mastery of language earned him great respect, an invitation to the White House, and the ear of the American public. In the mid-1900s, people like Martin Luther King, Jr. and Malcolm X continued Douglass's legacy through their own communication and speaking skills. These public figures and artists illustrate that those who can speak and write well readily earn people's respect, thus developing their own individuality and ability to fight for the success of their cause.

B

I have a very good friend who speaks really well. He is an example of how speaking correctly can lead to bigger and better things. He was always using words such as "like," "you know," "ain't." We all use these words when we talk to each other, but our teachers always tell us that adults in the business world don't like us to use slang like this. So, when my friend set up an appointment to interview for a summer job, we all told him not to use these words. He shrugged it off and didn't listen to us, and he didn't get the job. The second job he went to interview for was different. He didn't use those words, and he got the job. This goes to show that language can be the key to success.

So, which one did you pick as the AP English paragraph? We were fairly certain that you'd choose **A**. Now, here is the difficult part. **Why** did you pick it as the AP sample? Quickly list three reasons.

1. _____

2. _____

3. _____

Do your reasons include any of the following?

_____ clear thesis
_____ diction (word choice)
_____ sentence variety
_____ examples and details
_____ organization
_____ syntax (sentence structure)
_____ topic adherence
_____ vocabulary

You may not have used our exact words, but you probably did identify a couple of these points. Good, you DO know what an upper-level essay is. Now our job, *and yours*, is to provide opportunities for you to practice and develop the knowledge, skills, and techniques that will allow you to write a variety of successful AP English essays consistently.

What Actually Is an AP English Essay?

The College Board directly states that one of the goals of an AP English course is to have students become "practiced, logical, and honest writers." In other words, the AP English student is expected to read, think, plan, write, and revise so that the ideas presented are clear, appropriate, and effective for the chosen purpose and audience.

In general, an AP English essay will demonstrate the writer's ability to do the following:

1. Think through an idea.
2. Plan the presentation of his or her own claim (thesis, assertion, main point).
3. Draft a text that is logically organized to effectively support the writer's idea(s) and purpose.

The AP English student *must* be able to write a well-developed, timed essay, which is most often a critical analysis, argument, or exposition in response to a specific prompt. Those who create AP English courses and exams also expect the student writer to use the elements of syntax, diction, and rhetoric appropriate to the writer's purpose and audience.

Specifically, the student who elects to take the AP English Language or Literature exam in May will be required to do the following:

	ENGLISH LANGUAGE	ENGLISH LITERATURE
Part I	1 hour multiple choice	1 hour multiple choice
Part II	One essay that analyzes the rhetorical structure of a prose piece	One essay based on a given poetry selection(s)
		One essay based on a given prose passage
	One argumentative essay based on a given text	One essay that considers/analyzes/discusses a given subject/topic directly related to a major work of literary merit chosen by the student
	One synthesis essay based on a set of given sources about a specific subject	

What's the Difference Between the AP English Language and the AP English Literature Essays?

Basically, the AP English Language course concentrates on reading prose from various time periods, written to achieve many different purposes. The emphasis is on writing expository, analytical, and argumentative essays.

In general, Language essays are based on nonfiction works. You may be asked to do any of the following:

- Identify the author's purpose.
- Identify the audience.
- Identify and analyze the rhetorical strategies and/or language resources used by the author to achieve his or her purpose.

AND/OR

- Defend, refute, or qualify the author's position on a given subject.
- Create a synthesis essay.

In contrast, AP Literature students read a wide range of literary works of differing genres, and the assigned essays require the writer to focus on a given piece of literature, be it prose, poetry, or drama. The emphasis is on writing analytical, expository, and argumentative essays based on the literature.

Most often, literature essays are based on prose and poetry, although selections from drama may be included. For each, you may be asked to do any of the following:

- Analyze the techniques the author uses to produce a particular effect, reveal a character, develop a concept, etc., in the work.
- Compare and contrast two pieces of literature.

AND/OR

- Compose an essay based on a given topic that must be supported with specific references to a full-length literary work of your choice.

As we progress through this text, we look carefully at the various essay formats and requirements of each course.

What Are the Expectations of the AP English Essay?

> Before addressing this question, it is important to define two terms used throughout this book. The first is PROMPT. A prompt is the professional word that indicates the "question" on which your instructor or exam creator requires you to base an assigned essay. It is your essay assignment. The second is RUBRIC. A rubric is the professional word for a set of rating standards employed by the reader(s) of a given essay.

In Chapter 5 we work with the process of reading and working the essay prompts. Right now, let's take a close look at rubrics used for evaluating an AP English essay. For both Language and Literature the highly rated essays are assigned either a 9 or an 8. The middle-range essays receive anywhere from 7 to 5. (There are rare instances when a 7 could be said to be in the high range.) Those essays rated 4 to 1 are considered low range.

It is important to note that AP English essays on the AP exam are rated with numbers ranging from 9 to 1 for each of the exam's three essays. The AP English essays are also characterized as high, middle, and low range. With a specific formula, these scores are combined with the multiple choice score, and converted into an overall rating of the complete exam that ranges from 5 to 1.

 KEY IDEA

> A generic set of AP Language rubrics would look like this:

A 9 essay has all the qualities of an 8 essay, and the writing style is especially impressive, as is the analysis of the specifics related to the prompt and the text.

An 8 will effectively and cohesively address the prompt. It will analyze and/or argue the elements called for in the question. And, it will do so using appropriate evidence from the given text. The essay will also show the writer's ability to control language well.

A 7 essay has all the properties of a 6, only with a more complete, well-developed analysis/argument or a more mature writing style.

A 6 essay adequately addresses the prompt. The analysis and/or argument is on target and makes use of appropriate specifics from the text. However, these elements are less fully developed than scores in the 7, 8, 9 range. The writer's ideas are expressed with clarity, but the writing may have a few errors in syntax and/or diction.

A 5 essay demonstrates that the writer understands the prompt. The analysis/argument is generally understandable but is limited or uneven. The writer's ideas are expressed clearly with a few errors in syntax or diction.

A 4 essay is an inadequate response to the prompt. The writer's analysis/argument of the text indicates a misunderstanding, an oversimplification, or a misrepresentation of the given passage. The writer may use evidence that is inappropriate or insufficient to support the analysis/argument.

A 3 essay is a lower 4 because it is even less effective in addressing the prompt. It is also less mature in its syntax and organization.

A 2 essay indicates little success in speaking to the prompt. The writer may misread the question, only summarize the passage, fail to develop the required analysis/argument, or simply ignore the prompt and write about another topic. The writing may also lack organization and control of language and syntax. (***Note:*** **No matter how good the summary, it will never rate more than a 2.**)

A 1 essay is a lower 2 because it is even more simplistic, disorganized, and lacking in control of language.

KEY IDEA

> Although similar, there are specific differences between the Literature and Language rubrics. Here is a generic set of rubrics for an AP English Literature essay.

A 9 essay has all the qualities of an 8 essay, and the writing style is especially impressive, as is the relationship between the text and the subtext and the inclusion of supporting detail.

An 8 essay will effectively and cohesively address the prompt. It will refer to the appropriate text and provide specific and relevant references from the text to illustrate and support the writer's thesis as related to the prompt. The essay will indicate the writer's ability to perceive the relationship between text and subtext in a clear and mature writing style.

A 7 essay has all the properties of a 6, only with more well-developed analysis/discussion related to the prompt or a more mature writing style.

A 6 essay adequately addresses the prompt. The analysis/discussion is on target and makes use of appropriate references from the chosen literary work to support the thesis. However, these elements are less fully developed than scores in the 7, 8, or 9 range. The writer's ideas are expressed with clarity, but the writing may have a few errors in syntax and/or diction.

A 5 essay demonstrates that the writer understands the prompt's requirements. The analysis/discussion of the text and how it relates to the prompt is generally understandable, but it is limited or uneven. The writer's ideas are expressed clearly with a few errors in syntax and/or diction.

A 4 essay is an inadequate response to the prompt. The writer's analysis/discussion of the text and how it relates to the prompt indicates a misunderstanding, an oversimplification, or a misrepresentation of the chosen literary work. The writer may use evidence that is inappropriate or insufficient to support his or her thesis.

A 3 essay is a lower 4 because it is even less effective in addressing the text and how it relates to the prompt. It is also less mature in its syntax and organization.

A 2 essay indicates little success in speaking to the prompt. The writer may misread the question, choose an unacceptable literary work, only summarize the selection, fail to develop the required analysis, or simply ignore the prompt and write about another topic altogether. (*Note:* **No matter how good the summary may be, it will NEVER rate more than a 2.**)

A 1 essay is a lower 2 because it is even more simplistic, disorganized, off topic, and lacking in control of language.

Although each essay is rated on a scale of 9 to 1, your final AP English exam score is going to be a 5, 4, 3, 2, or a 1. If you'd like to transpose these numbers into letter grades, you could use the following as a guide.

ESSAYS	EXAM
9 = A+/A	5 = A
8 = A/A−	4 = B
7 = B+/B	3 = C
6 = B−/C+	2 = D
5 = C/C+	1 = F
4 = C−	
3 = D+	
2 = D	
1 = F	

So, if you receive a 7 on an AP English essay, you can think of it in terms of receiving a letter grade of B+ or an A−.

Is It Difficult to Write an Effective AP English Essay?

When we watch an athlete jumping hurdles, skiing down a precipitous slope, winning at Wimbledon, hitting a home run, or completing the marathon, we often say, "Wow, that sure looks easy." When we go to an art gallery and see a photograph by Ansel Adams or Annie Leibowitz or a painting by Pablo Picasso, we often hear people say, "I can do this. There's nothing to it."

However, doing something well is not always easy.

What is done well "appears" smooth and effortless. However, the observer is unaware of the hours, days, months, and sometimes years of practice, rehearsal, editing, and "tweaking" that go into the event or presentation.

The same is true of writing. Your favorite novelists, journalists, poets, playwrights, song writers, screenwriters, and essayists work their way through a process of observing, thinking, planning, prewriting, writing, and revision. Once their final draft is presented, you read it as a smooth, seamless piece of work. Try not to think of writing in terms of difficulty. Think of it as an ongoing process that becomes clearer and smoother with practice. Easy!

How Is This Book Going to Work?

IN THIS CHAPTER

Summary: Familiarize yourself with the function and purpose of this book

Key Ideas
- ✪ Create your personal writing profile
- ✪ Understand the basic training program
- ✪ Meet the graphics you'll encounter throughout the text

Creating Your Personal Writing Profile

This book will be your personal training manual for writing the AP English essay. Because we're going to be your personal AP writing trainers, we will ask you to do the first thing any good trainer would do. We're going to ask you to assess your needs. First, why are you here? What do you hope to gain from spending time and effort working your way through this text?

My primary goals are:

_____

_____

_____

_____

Make certain your goals are reasonable and realistic. For example, having a primary goal of winning the Nobel Prize in Literature during your year as an AP English student is not realistic—a terrific dream, but not a reasonable goal for this year.

The next step is to create a profile of you as a writer. To do this, you need to respond to the following statements.

My Personal Writing Profile

	Yes	No
I enjoy writing.	____	____
I find writing assignments intimidating.	____	____
I become nervous when I have to write a timed essay.	____	____
I have problems figuring out how to begin my essays.	____	____
I have difficulty organizing my ideas clearly.	____	____
I always revise my essays before handing in the final draft when possible.	____	____
I usually run out of time when writing a timed essay.	____	____
I have problems finding appropriate evidence in the given texts to support my thesis.	____	____
I often wander off the topic.	____	____
I often don't know when to stop writing.	____	____
I don't like to revise my writing.	____	____
I do my best writing under pressure.	____	____
I have taken other AP courses.	____	____
I have problems writing for specific purposes (i.e., exposition, analysis, argument)	____	____
AP English exam essay prompts scare me.	____	____
For my nontimed class essays, I always have one of my peers read my essay before I hand it in.	____	____

When I write an essay that allows for planning and revision, I usually receive a ____ high, ____ middle, or ____ low grade.

When I write a timed essay under controlled conditions, I usually receive a ____ high, ____ middle, or ____ low grade.

What frustrates me most about writing in general is _____

_____

_____

What frustrates me most about timed writing is _____

_____

_____

I do my best writing when _____

_____

_____

Take a few moments to consider your responses. If you answered these statements honestly, you have created a fairly accurate profile of yourself as a writer. Are you satisfied with your writing portrait? If you are, you don't need us—give this book to a friend! If you're not (to be honest, almost no one ever is), commit yourself to a training program—and invite a friend to work out with you.

About the Basic Training Program

Why the Basic Training Program?

We believe we have something unique to offer you. For over 25 years we have addressed the needs of AP students just like you, and we've had the opportunity to learn from these students. Therefore, the basic training program we offer in this book reflects genuine student concerns and needs. This is a student-oriented program. We will not overwhelm you with pompous language, mislead you with inaccurate information and tasks, or lull you into a false sense of confidence through cutesy shortcuts. We stand behind every suggestion, process and question we present. There is no busy work in this book.

This basic training program is designed to serve many purposes. It will:

- Clarify requirements for the AP English Essay for both Language and Literature
- Provide you with essay practice
- Show you models and rubrics on which you can model and evaluate your own work
- Anticipate and answer your questions
- Enrich your understanding and appreciation of the writing process
- Help you pace yourself
- Make you aware of the Five Steps to Mastering the AP English essay

We believe that reading should be an exciting interaction between you and the writer. You have to bring your own context to the experience and you must feel comfortable reaching for and exploring ideas. You are an adventurer on a journey of exploration, and we will act as your guides. We will set the itinerary, but you will set your own pace. You can feel free to "stop and smell the roses" or to explore new territory.

There are no tricks to critical thinking. Those who claim to guarantee you a 5 with gimmicks are doing you a disservice. No one can guarantee you'll get a 5. However, the reading and writing skills you will review, practice, and master will give you the very best chance to do your very best. You will have the opportunity to learn, to practice, and to master the critical thinking processes that can empower you to achieve your highest score.

Acting as your personal writing trainers, we have created a program to help you reach those goals you listed at the start of this section. **Remember, this book does *not* replace your AP English instructor, and it does *not* replace the work you must consistently and responsibly study and complete in your own AP English class.**

We highly recommend that you work your way through the entire book. However, be aware that this training program is designed to "pump up" all AP English students. Therefore, it will be up to you to make the important decisions about which chapters and sections of chapters to complete and how much time you will devote to any given chapter, section, or activity.

Reaching higher levels of achievement demands training, practice, and commitment. You've already taken the first step in your training to be an accomplished AP English essay writer. **Now, let's get to work.**

About the Icons Used in This Book

This book contains special graphic elements to help you find and identify important ideas, strategies, and tips. Here is a guide to the icons used:

 Key Idea: This icon points out a very important concept or fact that you should not pass over.

 Strategy: The strategy icon calls your attention to a problem-solving strategy that you may want to try.

 Tip: The tip icon indicates a hint you might find useful.

Workout: The workout icon identifies practice exercises within each chapter.

Important terms are printed in bold in this book and key information, definitions, and concepts are shaded. All this is designed to make this book as easy to use as possible, especially if you don't have much time to prepare for the AP exam.

STEP 2

Determine Your Readiness

CHAPTER 3

Review the Basics of Discourse

IN THIS CHAPTER

Summary: Distinguish among the four modes of discourse

Key Ideas
○ Understand the term "mode"
○ Practice with the individual modes

The Four Modes of Discourse

"Find a subject you care about and which you in your heart feel others should care about."
—Kurt Vonnegut, Jr.

As your writing trainers, we recommend that you begin with the basics. In any physical training program, if your personal trainer told you to do five sets of *crunches,* and you didn't have the foggiest idea what a *crunch* was, you would certainly ask, "What are you talking about?" Your trainer would not only explain what it is, but he or she would also demonstrate this exercise for you to practice. Then, you'd give it a try. Slowly at first, doing only a very few. Once comfortable, you would move on to the next step. This process also holds true with our writing training program.

The first set of basics is for you to become familiar with the **four modes of discourse.** Think of these activities as "breathing exercises" for AP English writers. Don't let the professional language throw you. **Remember that a mode refers to a method or form used, and discourse is the technical term for conversation. Therefore, a mode of discourse is simply a method a writer uses to have a conversation with a particular reader/ audience.**

You are already acquainted with the four modes of discourse. They are:

- **Exposition**—writing that explains or informs
- **Narration**—writing that tells a story
- **Description**—writing that appeals to the five senses
- **Argument/persuasion**—writing that presents a position in hopes that the reader will accept an assertion

So, there you have it, the four modes of discourse: exposition, narration, description, and argument.

As a warm-up exercise, let's look at four sentences that revolve around the same event. We're betting you can easily identify the mode of discourse of each statement.

Warm-Up Exercises

Warm-Up 1

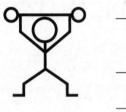

_____ **1.** Last night I took the train into the city with a couple of old friends to see Herman Overact as the lead in *The Crucible* at the Humongous Theater, and we had a terrific time.

_____ **2.** Herman Overact's performance in Arthur Miller's *The Crucible* is an acting event not to be missed.

_____ **3.** Herman Overact is playing the lead role in Arthur Miller's *The Crucible* at the Humongous Theater for the next six weeks.

_____ **4.** Last evening, the sold-out audience buzzed with excitement as it stared wide-eyed at the stage in rapt anticipation of the appearance of Herman Overact in Miller's *The Crucible*.

That was easy enough, wasn't it? But, wait a second. Let's take a closer look at these rather simple sentences. Didn't each of them contain information, and didn't each assume that the reader would accept what was stated? Yes, to both questions. If that's the case, how can you correctly identify each of the sentences as being a specific mode of discourse?

Be aware that most writing experts agree that **a writer rarely uses only a single mode of discourse.** However, even though more than one mode may be employed, there is a **dominant mode** that fits the author's specific purpose. The key word here is **purpose**—why the author composed each of these sentences. With this in mind, take another look at these four sentences. The primary purpose is what determines the primary mode of discourse. [Want to check your answers? (1) narration, (2) argument, (3) exposition, (4) description.]

Now, using this basic information, complete the following set: identify the dominant mode of discourse of each of the following excerpts. Read each carefully, keeping in mind that every author writes with a purpose. Whether you're dealing with an entire book or with a single sentence, **once you determine what the author's purpose is in a given context, you know what the dominant mode of discourse is.** Remember to ask yourself: What is the author's purpose?

Warm-Up 2

_____*Gertrude Stein liked to say that America entered the twentieth century ahead of the rest of the world. In 1933, in* The Autobiography of Alice B. Toklas, *she put it more strongly—that America actually created the new century.*

—R. W. B. Lewis, "Writers at the Century's Turn,"
appearing in *The Writing Life*

R. W. B. Lewis tells his readers about the thoughts of Gertrude Stein. Therefore, the dominant mode of discourse is **exposition** (although you might like to argue about what Ms. Stein had to say about America).

_____*My other hangout, strategically located near the front door, was under the porch, behind the blue hydrangeas. I could see the postman's hairy legs and black socks, the skirts of my mother's bridge friends, and sometimes hear bits of forbidden conversation. . . .*

—Frances Mayes, *Bella Tuscany*

In this short excerpt, Ms. Mayes attempts to have her readers sense her immediate surroundings and begin to feel her life as a child. This is an example of **description.**

_____*. . . we should not be surprised to find that [certain contemporary historians] have overlooked a tremendous contribution in the distant past that was both Celtic and Catholic, a contribution without which European civilization would have been impossible.*

—Thomas Cahill, *How the Irish Saved Civilization*

Here Thomas Cahill presents a very **arguable** assertion. You can be sure that there are people who will want to agree, disagree, or qualify his thesis.

_____*I, myself, was having a terrible time reading the paper, so yesterday morning, I went to Birmingham to get my eyes checked, and lo and behold, I had on Wilbur's glasses and he had on mine. We are getting different colored ones next time.*

—Fanny Flagg, *Fried Green Tomatoes at the Whistle Stop Cafe*

Fanny Flagg relates a brief episode that has a beginning, a middle, and an end. Although quite short; that's **narration.**

_____*So why do I write, torturing myself to put it down? Because in spite of myself I've learned some things. Without the possibility of action, all knowledge comes to one labeled "file and forget," and I can neither file nor forget.*

—Ralph Ellison, *Invisible Man*

Writing in the first person, Mr. Ellison is telling his reader about why he has to write. Although this excerpt appears in a full-length narrative, the dominant purpose of this selection is **exposition**.

• As your next warm-up exercise, identify the mode of discourse of each of the following.

Warm-Up 3

_____ *The cold air stung us and we played till our bodies glowed. Our shouts echoed in the silent street.*

—James Joyce, "Araby"

_____ *A buoy is nothing but a board four or five feet long, with one end turned up; it is a reversed school-house bench, with one of the supports left and the other removed.*

—Mark Twain, *Life on the Mississippi*

_____ *It is rather for us to be here dedicated to the great task remaining before us—that from these honored dead we take increased devotion to that cause for which they gave the last full measure of devotion—that we here highly resolve that these dead shall not have died in vain—that this nation, under God, shall have a new birth of freedom—and that government of the people, by the people, for the people, shall not perish from the earth.*

—Abraham Lincoln, "Address at the Dedication of Gettysburg Cemetery as a War Memorial"

_____ *The journey took about a week each way, and each day had my parents both in its grip. Riding behind my father I could see that the road had him by the shoulders, by the hair under his driving cap. It took my mother to make him stop. I inherited this nervous energy in the way I can't stop writing on a story.*

—Eudora Welty, *One Writer's Beginnings*

_____ *The law can only do so much in removing the burden of living vigilantly and responsibly, for our own sake and for our children's. So click off the Internet and go for a brisk walk. You look as though you could use some exercise.*

—George F. Will, "Sex, Fat and Responsibility," *Newsweek*, July 7, 1997

_____ *Beside us, on an overstuffed chair, absolutely motionless, was a platinum-blond woman in her forties, wearing a black silk dress and a strand of pearls. Her long legs were crossed; she supported her head on her fist.*

—Annie Dillard, *Teaching a Stone to Talk*

_____ *So I was a lucky child too. I played with a set of paper dolls called "The Family of Dolls," four in number, who came with the factory-assigned names of Dad, Mom, Sis, and Junior. . . . Now I've replaced the dolls with a life.*

—Barbara Kingsolver, "Stone Soup," *High Tide in Tucson*

_____ *I learned this, at least, by my experiment; that if one advances confidently in the direction of his dreams, and endeavors to live the life which he has imagined, he will meet with a success unexpected in common hours.*

—Henry David Thoreau, *Walden*

_____*Antigua used to have a splendid library, but in The Earthquake (everyone talks about it that way—The Earthquake; we Antiguans, for I am one, have a great sense of things, and the more meaningful the thing, the more meaningless we make it) the library building was damaged.*

—Jamaica Kincaid, *A Small Place*

_____*Partially covering his shaggy blond hair was one of those blue base-ball caps with gold braid on the bill and a sailfish patch sewn onto the peak. Covering his eyes and part of his face was a pair of those stupid-looking '50s-style wrap-around sunglasses.*

—Cherokee Paul McDonald, "A View from the Bridge,"
Sunshine Magazine

(You can find the answers in Appendix IV.)

You should give yourself time to practice this recognition skill as you read your academic assignments, as you peruse periodicals, and as you read for pure enjoyment. Stop every so often to ask yourself what the author's purpose is for the entire selection or for a specific portion of it. Then categorize it as exposition, narration, description, or argument. Why not invite a group of your peers to practice with you? As with any skill, the more you practice, the easier it becomes.

If you can recognize the modes of discourse, you should be able to identify them in your own writing. Because we're only doing basic exercises at this point, try your hand at composing a set of sentences, each of which revolves around the same subject but with a different purpose.

Warm-Up 4: Follow Our Lead

For example: Subject: my love of shoes

Exposition: I own several pairs of Kangaroo sneakers. They take up most of the shoe space in my closet. But, I can never have enough of them.

Narration: Yesterday, I saw an ad in the newspaper for a 60 percent sale on Kangaroo sneakers at the Bullseye department store. I can't resist either Kangaroo sneakers or a bargain, so I called two of my friends, and off we went. You would not believe the fun we had. Crowds, choices, credit cards, and lunch. My closet has never been so colorfully stuffed.

Description: My closet is boxed in by shoes. Shoes lined up on the top shelf, shoes straddling a rack on the floor, and shoes nestling in hanging pockets on the door. I like to think of it as my Kangaroo cage.

Argument: I've owned many different brands of sneakers, but none is as comfortable, colorful, long-wearing, and reasonably priced as Kangaroos. No other sneaker even comes close.

• Now, it's your turn.

My subject is _____

Exposition: _____

_____

_____

_____

Narration: _____

_____

_____

_____

_____

Description: _____

_____

_____

_____

_____

Argument: _____

_____

_____

_____

_____

If you have any doubt, or if you would like to check your "take" on your samples with the ideas of others, why not invite your peer group to complete this exercise and cross check and discuss them with each other? If you would like to post these samples, you can go to our Web site <**www.clearestideas.com**> and log them on for comments and identification from other students across the nation.

CHAPTER 4

Review the Basics of Rhetorical Construction

IN THIS CHAPTER

Summary: Become aware of the numerous rhetorical strategies available, including argument and synthesis

Key Ideas
- ✪ Understand the function of each of the major rhetorical strategies
- ✪ Practice with each of the major rhetorical strategies
- ✪ Check your work with each of the strategies

"Why do writers write? Because it isn't there."
—Thomas Berger

The second section of this book is like the stretching and aerobic exercises you do before you get down to the nitty-gritty fitness routine of building strength and flexibility and sculpting your muscles. So far you've been introduced to the first set of writing exercises in our training program: recognizing the four modes of discourse and writing examples of these (exposition, narration, description, and argument). Now, it's time to become familiar with the next set of writing aerobics.

Rhetorical Strategies

This second set of exercises will develop and strengthen your knowledge of rhetorical strategies.

Keep in mind that your familiarity with the professional terminology used in the course will contribute to your strength and flexibility when analyzing texts and writing about them.

The first term you must become comfortable with is **rhetorical strategy.** Simply, rhetoric is the method a writer or speaker uses to communicate ideas to an audience. And, you know what a strategy is; it's a plan or a course of action taken to reach a goal. Therefore, **a rhetorical strategy is the specific approach or approaches a writer employs to achieve an intended purpose.** Before going any further, it's important to understand what **purpose** is. **Purpose is the reason why you or any other person chooses to communicate with an audience—the goal, the intended effect.**

The basic purposes are:

- To inform
- To entertain
- To question
- To argue
- To elicit an emotional response

It doesn't matter whether it's Shakespeare, Strindberg, Steinbeck, or Sally Student; every author has a desire to explain, narrate, describe, or argue a specific topic. **HOW the writer accomplishes this is called a rhetorical strategy.**

Rhetorical strategies include:

- Cause/effect
- Classification/division
- Contrast/comparison
- Definition
- Description
- Exemplification
- Narration
- Process analysis
- Argument
- Synthesis

It doesn't matter how long or short the piece of writing is, an author will use one or more of these strategies to develop an overall purpose. One of the writer's first considerations MUST be the audience. For example, if a mathematician wanted to explain a mathematical principle to a general audience, the speaker or writer might contrast and compare several familiar objects or phenomena and narrate a personal story to illustrate the principle. However, if addressing a mathematics symposium, the speaker might choose to use process and analysis. It's all a matter of choice and knowing who the audience is.

In this chapter we work with the personal essay form and prewriting activities using the rhetorical strategies in writing personal essays. If you can perform these exercises well, you can duplicate the process in formal, academic essays. In addition, you will be more easily able to handle essay assignments that ask you to analyze a given text.

Exemplification

The most frequently used rhetorical strategy is **exemplification/example.** Whatever the subject, course, level of sophistication, or audience, examples are of utmost importance.

> **The fundamental ways a writer can illustrate, support, and clarify ideas include referring to a:**
>
> - sample
> - detail
> - person
> - typical event

Here are two very brief excerpts from longer works that illustrate the use of examples.

> *Even very inconsistent discipline may fit a child to live in an inconsistent world. A Balinese mother would play on her child's fright by shouting warnings against nonexistent dangers: "Look out! Fire! . . . Snake! . . . Tiger!" The Balinese system required people to avoid strange places without inquiring why.*
>
> —Margaret Mead, *A Way of Seeing*

The subject of this piece is obviously discipline, and Ms. Mead uses the example of a Balinese mother to illustrate how Balinese children are trained to avoid danger.

> *The new bread-and-circuses approach to mall building was ventured in 1985 by the four Ghermezian brothers . . . builders of Canada's $750 million West Edmonton Mall, which included a water slide, an artificial lake, a miniature-golf course, a hockey rink, and 47 rides in an amusement park known as Fantasyland.*
>
> —David Guterson, "Enclosed. Encyclopedic. Endured.
> The Mall of America," *Harper's Magazine*

Mr. Guterson's subject is a particular type of mall—the "bread and circus mall." He chooses to exemplify what this type of mall is with the West Edmonton Mall.

Our first exercise is a practice in recognizing the use of examples when you see it. It's easy AND quick. For our purposes, here, we are only going to concentrate on an excerpt. Just take your favorite magazine or newspaper and read what you ordinarily read in this periodical, and choose ONE of the articles to work with.

Warm-Up Exercises

Warm-Up 1

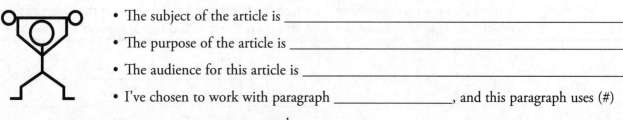

- The subject of the article is _____.
- The purpose of the article is _____.
- The audience for this article is _____.
- I've chosen to work with paragraph _____, and this paragraph uses (#) _____ examples.

Repeat this exercise with other readings until you feel familiar and comfortable with the task of recognizing examples when you see them. Also, be aware of the use of examples in your classroom texts. Remember that checking with a peer can be helpful to both of you.

This next exercise will work with your ability and flexibility to choose a subject and appropriate examples to illustrate it. Keep in mind that the only way a writer can honestly work with an idea is to choose something that is personally familiar or important. For example, suppose a writer chose the subject "my personal writing idiosyncrasies," with the purpose of illustrating these quirks to a general audience. What could be some examples of personal idiosyncrasies? How about biting nails, playing with hair, tapping a pen, scratching the head, crossing and uncrossing legs, saying "okay" at the ends of sentences, brushing back hair, humming while writing, doodling using only circles . . . You get the idea.

Okay, it's time for you to cite your examples.

Warm-Up 2

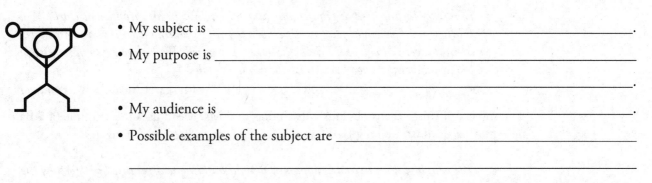

- My subject is _____.
- My purpose is _____
  _____.
- My audience is _____.
- Possible examples of the subject are _____
  _____
  _____
  _____

Easy, right? The next step is to choose which of the examples would best illustrate and support the subject and purpose.

> At this time, we would like to introduce you to "our writer" who will be authoring the writing samples we use throughout Chapters 3 and 4. He will be following the text and will complete the exercises just as you will. You will be able to read his responses and our comments on his writing.

So, our writer decides to use tapping a pen, brushing back hair, humming while writing, and doodling using only circles.

You already have your subject, purpose, audience, and possible examples in mind; now you need to choose which of these examples will BEST serve your subject/purpose. Most college level or AP essays are about 500 to 800 words long. You can't cover everything in an essay of this length. So, you have to choose to work with a limited number of examples. Remember, our writer chose four. Go back to your list of possibles. Given the limits of this personal essay, which examples would you choose that would BEST support and illustrate your subject and purpose?

- _____
- _____

- _____
- _____

Good, you've chosen your examples. Now, you need to make some decisions about organization.

This is your next exercise. How will you present your examples to your audience? You can choose from among the following organizational patterns:

✓ spatial (where it fits within a physical area)
✓ chronological (time sequence, from first to last)
✓ most important to least important
✓ the one I want to emphasize first
✓ the one I want to emphasize last
✓ least important to most important

Because our writer's purpose is to show the reader the quirky movements he goes through during the process of beginning to write, the choice is chronological order: brushing back hair, tapping the pen, doodling using circles, and finally humming while writing. Now, it's your turn.

Warm-Up 3

- I'm going to use the following organizational pattern: _____

_____

- In the order they will be used, my examples are: _____

_____

_____

_____

You're beginning to work up some writing steam now. Stay with it. Having chosen the organizational pattern and the examples that fit it, the writer is ready to construct the thesis statement. Let's review. We've decided on a subject, purpose, audience, appropriate examples, and their organization. How does the writer let the reader know all of this in a single sentence? **The writer creates a thesis statement or assertion.**

Not wishing to give away all of the examples at once, our writer composes the following thesis statement: ***Before actually putting pen to paper, I perform a peculiar prewriting ritual.*** This sentence does its job. We know the subject—quirky prewriting activity. We are aware of the purpose—illustrate the ritual. We don't know the specific examples that the writer will develop, but we are expecting some, and we are expecting these examples to be in chronological order because of the use of the word *Before*.

Following this demonstration, you should be able to construct a thesis statement that lets your chosen audience know the subject, sense the purpose, and recognize the organization of your examples.

- Here's my thesis: _____

_____

_____

_____

_____

Checklist

Does this statement clearly indicate the subject/topic? _____yes _____no

Does this statement give the reader a clear idea of the purpose? _____yes _____no

Does this statement indicate the actual examples that will be developed? _____yes _____no

Does this statement hint at the examples that will be used? _____yes _____no

Does this statement give the reader an idea of the organization? _____yes _____no

With the answers to each of these questions in mind, you may want to revise your thesis statement.

• Here is my revised thesis: _____

_____

_____

_____.

If you were to read the complete essay based on our writer's thesis, you would be asking yourself how well the writer performs each of the above exercises, and you would also need to ask yourself the following:

• Do the examples adequately support the thesis?
• Are the examples representative of indicated categories?
• Are the examples relevant to the purpose?

It doesn't matter for which class or for which topic, if the requirement is to use examples to develop a subject, you can use these exercises in developing your presentation. If you can easily perform these exercises for brief texts, you can easily perform them for longer texts.

Contrast/Comparison

Another rhetorical strategy available to you is **contrast/comparison (c/c).** Next to exemplification, contrast/comparison is the most widely used method of development for essays in the academic world. As an AP English student, you're already very familiar with comparison and contrast. **Contrast is interested in the differences, and comparison is interested in the similarities. It's rather important to know that the term _comparison_ is often used**

alone when referring to *both* types of analysis. (Yes, it is also analysis because you are taking something apart.) Here are three brief excerpts that illustrate contrast/comparison.

> *If there ever were two cultures in which differences of the [uses of space] are marked, it is in the educated (public school) English and the middle-class Americans. One of the basic reasons for this wide disparity is that in the United States, we use space as a way of classifying people and activities; whereas, in England, it is the social system that determines who you are.*
>
> —Edward T. Hall, *The Hidden Dimension*

Mr. Hall's subject is the use of space, and, in this instance, he chooses to **contrast** different strata of English and American culture.

> *Different as [Grant and Lee] were—in background, in personality, in underlying aspiration—these two great soldiers had much in common. Under everything else, they were marvelous fighters. Furthermore, their fighting qualities were really very much alike.*
>
> —Bruce Catton, "Grant and Lee: A Study in Contrasts,"
> *The American Story*

The subject for Mr. Catton is Grant and Lee. In this excerpt, he concentrates on the **similarities** between the two fighters.

> *Young men, in the conduct and manage of actions, embrace more than they can hold; stir more than they can quiet; fly to the end, without consideration of the means and degrees; pursue some few examples which they have chanced upon absurdity; care not to innovate, which draws unknown inconveniences; use extreme remedies at first; and, that which doubleth all errors, will not acknowledge or retract them; like an unready horse that will neither stop nor turn. Men of age object too much, consult too long, adventure too little, repent too soon, and seldom drive business home to the full period, but content themselves with a mediocrity of success.*
>
> —Francis Bacon, "Of Youth and Age"

The subject of Bacon's presentation is most probably youth and age, and in this excerpt the basis of **comparison** is the actions of young and older men with regard to success in business.

Our first contrast/comparison (c/c) exercise will involve your recognizing contrast/comparison when you see it. As with examples, this activity is quick and easy. Again, using your favorite periodical or newspaper, locate an article that seems to use c/c. Choose an excerpt from this article to work with.

Warm-Up 4

- The subject of the article is _____.
- The basis for comparison is _____.
- The purpose of the article is _____.
- The audience for this article is _____.

- I've chosen to work with paragraph _____.
- There are (#) _____ items being _____ compared _____ contrasted _____ compared & contrasted.
- These items are _____.

Repeat this exercise with other readings until you feel familiar and comfortable with the task of recognizing contrast/comparison when you see it.

> A clear comparison depends not only on choosing two things that can be compared, and being aware of your purpose and audience, but also on a balanced organization. There are THREE primary ways to organize a c/c presentation: subject-by-subject, point-by-point, and the combination approach.

The subject-by-subject pattern presents the details about the first item and then the details about the second. For example, our writer wants to compare two film directors. The areas to consider might include subject matter, cinematography, handling of actors, or handling of script. The subject-by-subject method presents all of the points about the first director and then all of the points about the second. An example might look like this:

I. First Director
   A. Subject matter   C. Handling of actors
   B. Cinematography   D. Handling of scripts

II. Second Director
   A. Subject matter   C. Handling of actors
   B. Cinematography   D. Handling of scripts

On the other hand, organizing the presentation point-by-point, the writer discusses one point at a time, going back and forth between the two. The outline might look like the following example:

I. Subject Matter   III. Handling of Actors
   A. First director   A. First Director
   B. Second director   B. Second director

II. Cinematography   IV. Handling of Scripts
   A. First director   A. First director
   B. Second director   B. Second director

In longer texts, a writer may choose to employ a combination of these two approaches. But, it is rare to see this method of presentation in shorter pieces of writing.

> No matter which organizational pattern you choose, make certain that you follow it throughout your essay.

This exercise will further develop your ability and flexibility to choose a subject for comparison, the areas to be compared, and the organization of the presentation. Remember to choose a subject that is familiar to you and of interest. You've seen what our writer has done; now it's your turn to practice this exercise.

Warm-Up 5

- I would like to compare _____ to _____.
- My purpose is to _____.
- My audience is _____.
- The basis for comparison is _____.
- The points I could include are _____

_____

_____

_____

Before planning the organization, make certain to choose points that are relevant to both items being compared. Circle those points that you have decided BEST suit your subject, basis for comparison, and purpose.

- I have decided to use the_____subject-by-subject_____point-by-point approach.
- Below is a brief outline.

_____

_____

_____

_____

_____

_____

> Don't work in a vacuum. Share your ideas with one or more of your AP classmates. Share them with your AP instructor. The more input you can gather the better. The more practice you can fit in the better.

Our writer chooses to employ the subject-by-subject method, and the resulting thesis statement is: **Sam Peckinpah and Ingmar Bergman are two film directors with completely different styles.** This thesis is on target. We know the subject—Sam Peckinpah and Ingmar Bergman. We know the basis for comparison—styles of directing. We are aware of the purpose—to compare the two directors. We don't know the specific organizational pattern at this time, but we could conclude that it will be subject-by-subject based on the way the sentence is worded.

Using this sample as a starting point, you should be able to construct a thesis statement that will let your reader know the subject, basis for comparison and the general purpose.

- Here is my thesis: _____

_____

_____

_____

Checklist

Does this thesis clearly indicate the subject for comparison? ____yes ____no

Does this statement indicate the basis for comparison? ____yes ____no

Does the statement give a general idea as to purpose? ____yes ____no

Does the statement give a hint of the organization? ____yes ____no

With the answers to each of these questions in mind, you may wish to revise your thesis.

- I've decided to revise my original thesis. Here is the revision:

_____

_____

_____

_____

_____.

If you were to read the complete c/c essay based on our writer's thesis, you would be asking yourself how well the writer performs each of the above exercises, and you would also need to ask yourself the following:

- Are the points for each subject developed adequately?
- Are the points relevant to the purpose and thesis?
- Is each of the body paragraphs balanced, using the pattern established in the first body paragraph?

Here's an exercise that may even prove to be helpful as you make decisions about which colleges you want to attend.

1. List those qualities you think are important in a college or university.
2. List the colleges that interest you.
3. Set up an organizational outline or chart just as you did in the last exercise.

You could choose to set up your comparison using college-by-college or quality-by-quality. Not only will you get further practice with the basics of contrast/comparison, but you will also be performing needed investigations to make an informed decision about your choice of a college or university.

Cause and Effect

You know about cause and effect. If you exercise your body every day, you will grow stronger and more flexible. If you perform the writing exercise diligently, your writing will become more clear, more mature, and more confident. **That's cause and effect (c/e). As a result of *A, B* occurs.** This linkage of events occurs along a timeline. Whether you're trying to figure out why your car is guzzling gas, the causes of road rage, the result of using hair spray as an insect repellent, the influence of one novelist on another, you are involved with cause and effect.

Below are a few brief excerpts that make use of cause and effect. When considering causes, keep the following in mind. There are

- primary causes,
- contributing causes,
- immediate causes,
- remote causes.

For example, if someone were to ask you why you're applying to college, you could respond in any number of ways:

✓ My parents are forcing me to apply. (immediate)
✓ My grandmother went to college. (remote)
✓ I want to have a successful career in ichthyology. (primary)
✓ I like the sound of "college graduate." (contributing)

The same situation holds true for effects or consequences of actions. There are primary and secondary effects as well as immediate and remote.

✓ My parents will be happy. (immediate)
✓ My kids will go to college. (remote)
✓ I will be the head of a new Marine World. (primary)
✓ People will respect me. (contributing)

Below are three brief excerpts which make use of cause and effect.

> *Some of this shift away from words—toward images—can be attributed to our ever-growing multilingual population. But for many people, reading is passé or impractical or, like, so totally unnecessary in this day and age.*
>
> —Linton Weeks, "The No-Book Report: Skim It and Weep,"
> *The Washington Post*, May 14, 2001

The subject of this passage is reading, and Mr. Weeks is interested in at least two reasons why the population is reading less.

> *Actually, no one can understand the action of Mrs. Parks unless he realizes that eventually the cup of endurance runs over, and the human personality cries out, "I can take it no longer." Mrs. Park's refusal to move back was her intrepid affirmation that she had had enough.*
>
> —Martin Luther King, Jr., *Stride Toward Freedom*

Martin Luther King, Jr.'s subject here is Mrs. Parks and the reasons she refused to move to the back of the bus. While we are not told in this selection the immediate cause of her refusal, we are certainly hearing Reverend King's belief as to the primary cause.

> *In Ireland, as food historian Reay Tannahill describes it, 'the potato famine meant more than food scarcity.' It meant no seed potatoes from which to grow next year's crop. It meant that the pig or cow which would normally have been sold to pay the rent had to be slaughtered, because there was nothing to fatten it on.*
>
> —Mary Talbot, "The Potato: How It Shaped the World,"
> *Newsweek*, October 12, 1991

In these sentences, Ms. Talbot's subject is the Irish potato famine and, not only its primary result, but also its secondary effects.

As we have been doing, this exercise will build your strength in recognizing the use of cause and effect when you see it. Take the periodical you read most often and find an ad that really captures your attention and probably makes use of cause and effect. (Just a hint—almost every ad in existence uses c/e.)

Warm-Up 6

- The subject of the ad is _____.

- The purpose of the ad is _____.

- The audience for this ad is _____.

- The ad is more interested in _____ cause(s) _____ effects(s)

- From what I can deduce, the cause(s) in this ad is/are _____

_____

_____

(Place a *P* above a primary cause, a *C* above contributing causes, *I* for immediate, and *R* for remote.)

- The ad indicates the following effect(s): _____

_____

_____

(Place a *P* above a primary effect, an *S* for secondary, an *I* for immediate, and an *R* for remote.)

> **TIP**
>
> We recommend that you also do this exercise using your own textbooks, especially in the sciences and history. You'll find that they are chock full of examples of cause and effect. This should provide you with myriad possibilities to practice, practice, practice, both alone and with your peers.

Okay, so you can easily recognize cause and effect when you see it. But, can you, as a writer, choose a subject and determine how you are going to examine cause and effect in relation to it? Well, work through this next exercise, and you'll no doubt find it easier to do this choosing and deciding.

For example, our writer has chosen a subject—vegetarianism—and has decided to inform the reader about the effects that becoming a vegetarian has had on his life. Given this subject, purpose, and audience, the best course of action would be to emphasize **effect**. The question remains whether to choose one effect or several. To start the process, our writer lists all those effects which immediately come to mind: old friends and family think I'm weird; I become very good friends with my neighborhood greengrocer; I feel better; I have less guilt about food; I save money; I sleep better; I no longer fear being a vegetarian; I make new friends; I lose weight; I create my own vegetarian Web site; I add new shelves of vegetarian cookbooks to my library; my refrigerator looks like a large green salad. . . . Need we go on?

Knowing that a decision has to be made, our writer spends some time thinking about the list of consequences. "Do I want to concentrate only on the primary effect? Do I want to develop the primary, plus the secondary? Or, do I want to consider the immediate effect and forget about the remote ones?" The choice is made! Our writer will concentrate on just one effect—the response of his friends and family. This will entail both immediate as well as remote consequences. And, our writer is aware not to settle for one cause or effect when there could be more

Now you try it. We'll give you the subject this time. Your subject is **the popularity of a TV show, movie, rock star, book. (Choose one.)**

Warm-Up 7

- My specific subject is _____.
- My audience is _____.
- My purpose is _____.

    I'm going to **emphasize** _____ cause, _____ effect, _____ causes, _____ effects.

- I believe I'll use one or more of the following in relation to what I decided to emphasize:

    _____ primary cause   _____ primary effect
    _____ contributing cause(s)   _____ secondary effect(s)
    _____ immediate cause   _____ immediate effect
    _____ remote cause(s)   _____ remote effect(s)

Don't write that thesis statement just yet. You still need to make some decisions about your organization. Do you want to present your ideas in chronological order, from most to least important, or vice versa? Our writer has decided to use chronological order. What arrangement will you use to organize your ideas?

_____ chronological _____ most to least important _____ least to most important

It's now time to write that thesis statement. Our writer thinks, doodles for a while, scribbles a bit, writes a first draft, thinks, and finally writes the following revised thesis: ***My family and friends no longer see me as the potential Himalayan hermit they first imagined when they became aware that I had become a vegetarian.*** Notice the indicators of chronology: *no longer, first imagine, when.* Notice also that this sentence gives the reader fair warning that what follows is going to center on the effect on family and friends.

Okay. You have all of the needed information about your own subject in front of you. Your job is to compose your own thesis statement for a cause and effect presentation.

Warm-Up 8

- My initial thesis is _____

_____

_____

_____

_____ .

Checklist

- Does this thesis statement clearly indicate the subject? ____yes ____no
- Does this statement make it clear to the reader that this is a cause and effect presentation? ____yes ____no
- Does the statement give the reader a general idea as to purpose? ____yes ____no
- Does the statement give the reader an idea as to what the emphasis will be? ____yes ____no
- Does the statement give an indication what the organization will be? ____yes ____no

With these answers in hand, you may want to revise your original thesis statement.

- Here's my revised thesis: _____

_____

_____

_____

_____ .

If you were to read a complete cause and effect essay based on our writer's thesis, as in any analysis of a text, you would ask yourself how and how well the author performs the tasks you have been practicing. You would also need to ask yourself the following.

- Have the causes and effects been clearly connected to the subject?
- Given the subject and purpose, are there any obvious or needed causes or effects that are missing?
- Is the organization appropriate for the subject and purpose?

Classification and Division

Classification and division are true work horses of rhetorical strategies. You can find yourself using classification and division for almost any purpose and for almost any subject. **Basically, classification is the process of grouping items together that share important characteristics. Classification goes from specific to general, from small groups or examples to larger, more general categories. Division goes from the whole (general) to the parts (specific categories, groups, examples).** It may be easier to visualize the difference between the two if we take a look at a football team. If I wanted to discuss the **types** of football teams, I would be dealing with **classification**. However, if I wanted to examine the **organization** of a football team or who is on the team, I would be using **division**.

Here are two brief excerpts that use classification and/or division.

Aaron takes me only to art films. That's what I call them, anyway: strange movies with vague poetic images I don't always understand, long dreamy movies about a distant Technicolor past, even longer black-and-white movies about the general meaninglessness of life. . . . Pete takes me only to movies that he thinks have redeeming social value.

—Susan Allen Toth, "Cinematypes," *Harper's Magazine*, 1980

Here is a rather interesting passage. Although the subject of the entire essay might very well be this writer's two friends and informing the reader how she relates to each, this particular section is about the types of movies the two friends like: art movies and movies with "redeeming social value." And, even though most instructors will advise you to choose a classification principle that has more than two categories associated with it, in this instance, Ms. Toth is referring to only two. Each of these will probably have subclasses.

I spend a great deal of my time thinking about the power of language—the way it can evoke emotion, a visual image, a complex idea, or a simple truth. Language is the tool of my trade. And I use them all—all the Englishes I grew up with.

—Amy Tan, "Mother Tongue," *Threepenny Review*, 1990

It's quite obvious from this very short bit of text that Ms Tan's subject is language, her purpose is to inform, and her classification is going to revolve around several types of English.

Now, you try it. Following our routine, the first classification exercise will provide you with practice recognizing classification when you see it. Take a close look at your history and science textbooks. We guarantee that you will find examples of classification in these books. Because you're using a textbook, the purpose is obviously to inform a student audience.

Warm-Up 9

- I chose to look in the following textbook: _____.
- I located one, and its subject is _____.
- The basis for the classification (classification principle) is _____
_____.
- There are_____ groups within this classification principle.

Don't stop with just one sample; try many, and get your AP classmates to do some with you. They're easy to find and will give you and your peers valuable practice.

Not only do you need to be aware of the above guidelines, but you must also be certain that your groupings are:

✓ **Uniform**—This is the principle on which the groups are created. It's the umbrella under which all of your categories fit.

✓ **Consistent**—All the categories truly fit into the principle you've created.

✓ **Exclusive**—No category overlaps another.

✓ **Complete**—All of the examples you're including in your presentation are grouped into the appropriate category based on your purpose

As an example, suppose our writer decides to compose a humorous essay that classifies certain types of dogs.

✓ The basis for the classification will be how dogs view themselves in relation to their owners.
✓ The categories will be: (1) those who see themselves as king or queen, (2) those who see their owners as king or queen, and (3) those who see themselves as court jesters.
✓ We may have a problem with number 3. Is it possible that 3 overlaps with 2? Yes. Our writer realizes that a court jester is under the control of the king or queen. So, it will be a subclass of 2.

Try this easy one yourself. Consider your friends as the subject for a classification essay.

Warm-Up 10

- My subject is "my friends."
- My purpose is _____.
- My audience is _____.
- My classification principle is _____
  _____.
- My categories are: _____
  _____.

Checklist

I've checked to see that all the categories fit into my principle of classification.

____yes ____no

I've made certain no category overlaps with any other. ____yes ____no

The next step in prewriting the classification essay is to consider the organization and the details. Think about how to present the material. Based on purpose and audience, decide among chronological, logical (how the groups relate to each other and to the classification principle), least to most important, or vice versa. That done, choose which details will BEST support the thesis and purpose.

With this information in mind, our writer chooses the logical approach for organizing his material and decides that the details will all revolve around relationships—dog to owner and owner to dog. Our writer creates this thesis statement: ***Anyone who has ever owned or been owned by a dog is familiar with the two basic categories of man's best friend: dogs who believe they are kings and dogs who believe their owners are kings.*** The juxtaposition of dog, ownership, and king places the subject and principle of classification into a humorous vein for a general audience. Rightfully, the reader will be expecting the writer to provide subgroups and appropriate examples within each subgroup.

You're next. Go back to your prewriting notes above. Consider that information, plus the need to decide on an organizational pattern and appropriate details.

Warm-Up 11

- I've decided to use the following as my organizational pattern _____ chronological _____ logical _____ least to most important

- I chose this organizational pattern because _____

_____.

- Some of the appropriate subgroups I should include are: _____

_____

_____

_____

- This is the first draft of my thesis statement: _____

_____

_____

_____

_____

Carefully read your thesis and ask yourself if the purpose is clear, if the subject and principle of classification are given, as well as an indication of the organization and possible subgroups. Once you've done this, ask yourself whether or not the first draft of your thesis statement needs to be revised. If it does, rewrite below.

- This is my revised thesis: _____

_____

_____

_____

_____.

Process Analysis

If you were to take a careful look at the work you've just done in the last section of this chapter, you could not help but notice that we provide you with instructions about how to do the prewriting work for the classification/division essay. This is a demonstration of a process that just happens to be the next rhetorical strategy we will develop. **Process analysis is the method of describing how to perform a task or explaining how something works by breaking it down into the chronologically ordered steps that lead to the goal.** We use this strategy quite often, from telling someone how to set the VCR, to cookbook instructions on baking a cake; from telling your friend how to get a particular teacher to allow him to hand in a paper late, to explaining to your parents why you did not

do well on a math exam. You might have noticed that there may be **two types of process analysis,** and you would be right. Each serves a specific purpose.

✓ Process analysis that is **directive** provides step-by-step instructions.
✓ Process analysis that is **informative** explains how something works or is done.

Take a look at the following excerpts that use process analysis.

> *If you don't know where to begin [the letter], start with the present moment: I'm sitting at the kitchen table on a rainy Saturday morning. Everyone is gone and the house is quiet. Let your simple description of the present moment lead to something else, let the letter drift gently along.*
>
> —Garrison Keillor, *We Are Still Married*

Mr. Keillor's subject is how to write a letter. From this brief excerpt, it seems the process analysis will be **directive** because the author is beginning to give the chronologically ordered steps for writing a letter.

> *In personal situations, complaints may come the way of vague statements. . . . While there may be more serious relationship issues at hand, there is a specific way to help the situation. What you want to do is to have him get as specific as possible about what is bothering him.*
>
> —David Lieberman, *Get Anyone to Do Anything:*
> *Never Feel Powerless Again–With Psychological Secrets*
> *to Control and Influence Every Situation*

Even the title of this author's book gives a clear indication that we are dealing with process. Notice that the writer uses the phrase "there is a specific way." This is a clue that this part of the text is using a **directive** process analysis. And, from other wording in this selection, informative analysis is also possible.

It's time for you to try recognizing process analysis. As we've said before, you can find examples of this strategy almost anywhere. Why not use your textbooks, especially in such "lab courses" as biology, chemistry, or physics. That's easy pickin's. For more sophisticated practice, try locating examples in the magazines and periodicals you read. For every example you can pinpoint, determine the following:

Warm-Up 12

• The text I found this example of process analysis in is _____
_____.

• The subject is _____.

• The audience is _____.

• The purpose is (What is the reader supposed to do with this information?): _____
_____.

• The process analysis is primarily ____directive ____informative.

Our now famous writer is in a sarcastic mood and has decided to write a process essay about drivers' tests. Because this will be for a general audience, and because the writer wants to be a bit humorous, the specific subject will be how NOT to pass a driver's test. Going for humor, our author will use a directive approach.

You're up! Think about important events in your life: holidays, birthdays, other celebrations. What processes are involved? Think about activities in your life, those you like and those you dislike: dining with your parents' friends, meeting with your date's parents, dealing with an angry teacher, enjoying a baseball game, eating pizza, and so on.

Warm-Up 13

- My subject is _____.
- My audience is _____.
- My purpose is _____.
- My approach will be____directive____informative.

Whether it's directive or informative, the process analysis should be in sequential (chronological) order. Aside from sequence, you also need to consider how much information your reader already has. This will determine how much or how little detail to provide. For example, if we're writing about maintaining Harley–Davidsons, the type and amount of information we need to give an audience of motorcycle enthusiasts is quite different from the details needed for nonenthusiasts. (This would also strongly influence the purpose and choice of process analysis.)

Our writer knows that his audience is one that has experience as drivers; therefore, they have a good idea what a driver's test is like. He decides to use the following steps in sequence.

1. Be on time.
2. Be familiar with your test car.
3. Greet your inspector.
4. Listen to the instructor at all times.
5. Keep your eyes on the road.
6. Keep your hands on the wheel.
7. Precisely follow the inspector's instructions.
8. Say a prayer of thanks when you finish.

Step right up! You know your subject, audience, and purpose. Now, consider how much your readers already know about your subject. This should give you an idea about the type of information and how much added detail you must provide.

Warm-Up 14

- The steps in the order I would like to use them are:

   1. _____
   2. _____

3. _____

4. _____

5. _____

6. _____

7. _____

8. _____

You don't have to use all eight steps; in fact, you might very well use fewer or even more. This is all dependent on your purpose, audience, and length of presentation.

Once this is completed, it's time to write the thesis statement for the process analysis. Our writer has thought about all of the prewriting activities so far and has written the following thesis: ***Having been through the trials, tribulations, and pitfalls of this American rite of passage, I believe I'm wise enough to advise prospective highway jockeys how NOT to pass their driver's test.*** Drivers' tests, a humorous purpose, a general audience, and a directive process analysis are all indicated in this sentence.

You can do this. Using the information from the prewriting you've already developed, try your hand at composing the thesis statement for your process analysis essay.

Warm-Up 15

• Here's the first draft of my thesis: _____

_____

_____

_____

_____.

Checklist

As you have done with the previous strategies, carefully reread your thesis and complete each of the following:

My subject is clearly indicated.____yes____no

It's easy to see what my purpose is.____yes____no

It is obvious that the process analysis will be directive or informative. ____yes____no

This thesis statement gives the reader a clear idea that what follows will be a process analysis essay.____yes____no

Once you've answered these brief questions, you can easily see whether or not your first draft needs revision.

• Here's the second draft of my thesis statement. _____

_____

_____

_____

_____

_____ .

Remember to practice often and with your classmates. Feedback from others taking the AP English course can be of great help in honing your skills.

Definition

Now that you are up to speed with the all of the rhetorical strategies we've had you working with, you're ready to refine your skills with the strategy of definition. **Basically, a definition is the meaning of a word.** However, you know and we know that it's not this simple. For example, we've all been in situations where we've said to someone, "I don't know whatyou mean." And, we all know that the person who defines the word for us can choose to be **denotative/objective, acting like a dictionary, or connotative/subjective, giving you her personal meaning and relationship with the word.** So, if I asked you what the word *educated* means, you could provide a definition as if you were *Webster's Dictionary* (denotative/objective), or you could define it the way you personally see and relate to it (connotative/subjective).

Here are two excerpts by writers who are making use of definition.

> *Being a hippie is not about putting a flower in your hair and dancing around in your bare feet. Being a hippie means approaching life's obstacles in a way that promotes freedom, peace, love, and respect for our earth and all of mankind.*
> —Katherine Marie DiFillippo, "Love or Haight,"
> *Making Sense, A New Rhetorical Reader*

Based on these two sentences, it is obvious that Ms. DiFillippo's subject is the definition of the word *hippie*. It is also quite clear that she is developing a **connotative/subjective** definition of the term.

> *. . . in a very real sense, crime is a legal concept: what makes some conduct criminal, and other conduct not, is the fact that some, but not others, are "against the law."*
>
> *Crimes, then, are forbidden acts. But they are forbidden in a special way.*
> —Lawrence M. Friedman,
> *Crime and Punishment in American History*

This excerpt from Mr. Friedman's book clearly indicates the subject to be the meaning of the concept *crime*. At this point, it seems that the definition is **denotative/objective.**

If you take a close look at textbooks, you will find many, many examples of definition. However, the real challenge is finding examples of definition used in TV commercials and in the ads in the regular reading you do of magazines and periodicals.

Here's a good idea. Collect examples of the various rhetorical strategies that you locate in your own reading. Identify each and underline key words or phrases that support your identification. You could also do this with ads you find in magazines. Place all of these excerpts in an envelope that you tape inside the back cover of this book. It will prove to be a marvelous review tool for you.

The objective and subjective distinctions aren't the only things you need to be aware of when dealing with definition. You must consider the following.

✓ Purpose (Do you want to inform or to argue a point?)
✓ Audience (What do your readers know about this subject?)
✓ Tone (Do you want to be serious, humorous, or a combination of the two?)
✓ Developing the definition (Have you used one or more of the following?)

  ○ Examples
  ○ Description
  ○ Comparisons
  ○ Negative comparisons
  ○ Classification or division
  ○ Cause and effect
  ○ Narration
  ○ Historical background

Let's assume that you have made all of the necessary decisions reviewed above. Where do you go from here? The first thing you must do is to construct a brief definition that states the word or concept, the class or group to which it belongs, and how it is different from all others in that category.

WORD/CONCEPT +	CLASS +	DIFFERENTIATION
For example: SUV +	is a car +	that serves as a combination family car, pick-up truck, and sports vehicle.

Therefore, the definition is: *An SUV is a car that serves as a combination family car, pick-up truck, and sports vehicle.*

Our well-practiced writer has decided to define the term *bugdust.* Term = bugdust, class = expletive, differentiation = original, personally invented so that the user can avoid using unacceptable four-letter words in tense situations. Our writer has also chosen a subjective, humorous approach to inform a general audience, and will use examples, cause and effect, and historical background to develop the definition.

Step up to the plate. Now, you choose a subject. How about choosing a word that has special meaning only to you, or to you and your family or friends? How about a current slang word?

Warm-Up 16

- The word/phrase I've chosen to define is _____.
- The class of the word is _____.
- The differentiation is _____

_____

- My audience is _____.
- My purpose is to____inform, or____argue a point.
- My tone will be____serious,____humorous, or____a combination of both.
- I would probably use one or more of the following to develop my definition:

____ Examples
____ Description
____ Comparisons
____ Negative comparisons
____ Classification and/or division
____ Cause and effect
____ Narration
____ Historical background

Our writer has carefully thought about the subject and has written the following thesis statement: ***The expletive, Bugdust, is my personal substitute for the ever-popular, overused four-letter vulgarities.*** All of the needed information is present in this sentence. The reader is told the subject, the type of definition, and a very brief meaning of the term

Here's your chance to come up with an appropriate thesis statement for your own definition essay. Remember the activities you practiced above.

- My thesis statement is: _____

_____

_____

_____

Checklist

Have you made it clear to your reader what the parameters are for your term?____yes ____no

Is it also clear that your presentation will be objective or subjective? ____yes ____no

If you've answered "no" to either of these questions, you will need to revise.

- My revised thesis is: _____

_____

_____

_____

_____

Description

We've saved two of the most creative rhetorical strategies until now so that you would have a great many skills to pull from your writing routine. The first of these is **description. A writer uses description to recreate a person, place, thing, or idea in ways that appeal to the senses.** We use description everyday in many ways, from readings in textbooks to telling a friend over the phone about a new jacket, from telling the insurance company about the damages to a car, to recreating a feeling of happiness.

The description can be either informative or impressionistic/evocative.

- An informative description is the one that is factual, practical, and to the point. (The house is a two-story, white colonial with a black roof, black shutters on the windows, and a red front door.)
- The impressionistic/evocative description appeals to the reader's senses, intellect and emotions. (The wind moaned as if the night were in pain.)

Carefully read the following excerpts that make use of description.

> I can call back the solemn twilight and mystery of the deep woods, the earthy smells, the faint odors of the wild flowers, the sheen of the rain-washed foliage, the rattling clatter of drops when the wind shook the trees, the far-off hammering of woodpeckers and the muffled drumming of wood pheasants in the remoteness of the forest, the snapshot glimpses of disturbed wild creatures scurrying through the grass—I can call back the prairie, and its loneliness and peace, and a vast hawk hanging motionless in the sky, with its wings spread wide and the blue of the vault showing through the fringe of their end feathers. I can see the woods in their autumn dress, the oaks purple, the hickories washed with gold, the maples and the sumachs luminous with crimson fires, and I can hear the rustle made by the fallen leaves as we plowed through them. I can see the blue clusters of wild grapes hanging among the foliage of the saplings, and I remember the taste of them and the smell. I know how the wild blackberries looked, and how they tasted, and . . . the pawpaws, the hazelnuts, and the persimmons; and I can feel the thumping rain upon my head, of hickory nuts and walnuts when we were out in the frosty days . . .
>
> —Mark Twain, *Autobiography*

From the very first line, the reader is taken into the "deep woods" of Mark Twain's memory. The author vividly recreates this woodland scene by means of **impressionistic/evocative** description such as "snapshot glimpses of disturbed wild creatures," "solemn twilight," "sumachs luminous with crimson fires."

> And this is how I see the East. I have seen its secret places and have looked into its very soul; but now I see it always from a small boat, a high outline of mountains, blue and afar in the morning; like faint mist at noon; a jagged wall of purple at sunset. I have the feel of the oar in my hand, the vision of the scorching blue sea in my eyes. And I see a bay, a wide bay, smooth as glass and polished like ice, shimmering in the dark. A red light burns far off upon the gloom of the land, and the night is soft and warm. We drag at the oars with aching arms, and suddenly a puff of wind, a puff faint and tepid and laden with strange odors of blossoms, of aromatic wood, comes out of the still

*night—the first sigh of the East on my face. That I can never forget. It was impalpable
and enslaving, like a charm, like a whispered promise of mysterious delight.*

—Joseph Conrad, "The East"

Joseph Conrad is also recreating a locale from his memory. This scene is of his recollections
of the "East." Notice phrases like "impalpable and enslaving, like a charm," "jagged wall of
purple at sunset." These are just two examples of the **impressionistic/evocative** description
used throughout this excerpt.

Both of these authors illustrate what a vivid description can be. Not only have they
chosen their subjects with care, but they have also completed several other important steps
in composing a successful description. First, it is obvious that they chose a dominant
impression they want their readers to feel. For Twain, it is a connection to nature, and
for Conrad, it is a sense of strangeness and mystery. Second, they each carefully chose their
organizational pattern. This pattern can be any of the following.

✓ Chronological (time sequence)
✓ Spatial (positions from a particular point of view)
✓ Most noticeable feature (details in relation to this feature)
✓ Importance (details used to reinforce the most important feature) **Both Twain and
Conrad use a spatial organization.**

To give yourself practice recognizing these different types of description, the dominant
impression, and the methods an author can employ to create a description, try a few of the
following:

• Find an interesting photograph in a magazine or newspaper.
  Determine the subject and ask yourself:
  ○ What is the dominant impression?
  ○ Do you think the photographer intended to be factual or evocative?
  ○ Is the photograph emphasizing sequence, location, a very noticeable feature, an impor-
    tant feature?
  ○ You can also do this with your own photographs. Search your albums and photograph
    collections. We're certain you'll find many from which to choose.
• As you're reading your favorite periodical, notice description. Choose a specific excerpt
  and ask the same questions as above: subject, dominant impression, type, organization.
  You can also do this with the books you're reading outside of class or for class assignments.

As for writing a description, suppose our writer chooses to describe a traffic jam on the
way to entering a tunnel. The writer makes the following decisions:

✓ The audience will be a general one.
✓ The purpose will be to evoke the feeling of being caught in the jam. Therefore, impres-
  sionistic description is in order.
✓ The organizational pattern will be spatial.
✓ The dominant impression will be anger and frustration.

Take your position. Choose a person, place, thing, idea to describe. Make the types
of choices our writer did above. Perhaps you'd like to describe your room, a favorite place,
riding your favorite amusement park ride, winning a game, meeting your date for the first
time, your favorite car, a frustrating experience, or so on.

Warm-Up 17

- My subject is _____.

- I will create a description that is _____ informative _____ evocative.

- The dominant impression will be _____.

- My organization pattern will be _____ chronological _____ spatial _____ most noticeable

  feature _____ most important feature.

Once these choices are made, you need to consider the language you will need to create the description. If you wanted to write an informative description of a house, you would use **objective and denotative language**—in other words, language that keeps the writer's personal feelings, and so forth, out of the situation. Just the cold, hard facts are given, as in scientific journals, hard news articles, and accident reports. On the other hand, if you wanted to interject your personal attitudes, and so forth into a depiction of a house, you would choose primarily subjective and connotative language. A 1955 Chevy convertible can be a vintage, prized possession, or it can be an old, scrappy jalopy. **Choices depend on purpose and audience.**

Although a description can make use of both objective and subjective language, if an author employs subjective language, this can include **figurative language**, such as

- ✓ Direct comparison (metaphor)
- ✓ Indirect comparison (simile)
- ✓ Concrete words
- ✓ Imagery
- ✓ Onomatopoeia

Our writer is "champing at the bit" to create his description of the traffic jam leading into a tunnel. Because the preliminary choices have all been made, all he needs to do is to compose the thesis statement. ***Here I am caught for the umpteenth time in the never-ending traffic jam that leads to the Lincoln Tunnel. I usually tap my fingers on the steering wheel, listen to the radio, and kind of space out. However, this time I feel like a piece of meat slowly being forced through a grinder to form a sausage.*** Okay. This is one unhappy, frustrated, and hopeless commuter. It is quite obvious from the predominantly subjective, connotative, and figurative language that this is an impressionistic description organized in a spatial pattern.

Practice time! Using your own prewriting information, compose the first draft of your thesis statement for your descriptive essay.

Warm-Up 18

- My thesis is: _____

  _____

  _____

  _____

  _____.

Checklist

Carefully reread your thesis statement and answer the following questions:

- My subject is clearly indicated. ____yes ____no

- It is clear that my description will be predominantly ____ informative, ____impressionistic.

- My reader gets a clear indication of the dominant impression I'm going to work toward.

  ____yes ____no

- I've also indicated to my reader that the description will be predominantly ____ objective, ____ subjective.

- I've given my reader an indication what my organizational pattern will be. ____yes ____no

If you've answered "no" to any of these questions, you need to revise your thesis.

- Here is my revised thesis statement: _____

  _____

  _____

  _____

  _____.

Narration

KEY IDEA

Our next-to-last rhetorical strategy is **narration.** Everyone loves a story and loves to be told stories. It's in our genes. It's one of those things that makes us human. And, it is one of those writing strategies that can really make an assertion "come alive." **In narration, a writer tells or retells a sequence of events within a particular time frame for a specific purpose.** You know the routine. A story needs a beginning, a middle, and an end. As a rhetorical strategy, a narrative can be of any length, from a simple anecdote to the complete presentation.

No matter what the purpose, time frame, or sequence, a narration needs a **point of view.** The choices include:

- First person (I, we, us),
- Stream-of-consciousness, an off-shoot of first person, allows the reader to enter the mind of the narrator and be privy to the working of his mind.
- Third person (he, she, they, them).
  - with third person objective, the narrator acts as a reporter;
  - with third person omniscient, the narrator knows all.

Can you identify the characteristics of narration we've just mentioned in each of the excerpts below?

> *One day General Littlefield picked our company out of the whole regiment and tried to get it mixed up by putting it through one movement after another as fast as we could execute them: squads right, squads left . . . etc. In about three minutes one hundred*

and nine men were marching in one direction and I was marching away from them at a right angle of forty degrees, all alone. "Company, halt!" shouted General Little-field. "That man is the only man who has it right!" I was made a corporal for my achievement.

—James Thurber, "University Days,"
My Life and Hard Times

In this first person anecdote, Mr. Thurber relates a personal tale that has a beginning, a middle, and an ending.

My guardian angel was a light sleeper. He saved me from speeding cars, playground fights, and mercury splashing on my face. That was in fifth grade when we stole balls of mercury from the science teacher to shine coins and belt buckles. Finished, we closed one eye and flung the mercury at each other and giggled all the way to lunch.

—Gary Soto, "The Guardian Angel," *A Summer Life*

Mr. Soto uses first person to narrate this brief episode that is obviously part of a much longer work. Even in its brevity, the story has a beginning, a middle, and an ending.

 Writing a narrative demands its own special prewriting routines. Before composing a narrative, you need to decide on each of the following:

- The point to be made (commonly termed the *theme*)
- The point of view
- The temporal basis for the story (setting)
  - the time
  - (plot) to the major sequence of events
- The major sequence of events
- The characters/people in the story
- The primary tension of the story (conflict)
- The major details necessary for the story

In James Thurber's first person anecdote, a boot camp event is used to illustrate the old adage: the best laid plans often go awry. The time is the recent past, the setting a military encampment, and the sequence of events is quite clear. The tension centers on whether or not the general will succeed in confusing the company of men to whom he has given a series of marching directions. Although brief, details of the types of orders given, the number of men, dialogue and the indication of time, all contribute to the liveliness and believability of the story.

Mr. Soto tells his brief, first person episode to illustrate the childhood obliviousness of danger and repercussions of danger. The time is the recent past, the setting an elementary school science room, and the sequence of events is logical and clear. The tension centers around the fifth grade narrator and his friends playing with the dangerous metal—mercury. Soto's details in this very short tale contribute to the sense of place and childhood abandon.

You are not going to write a complete narrative in this activity, but you will do some of the prewriting necessary to compose it successfully. Our writer has chosen to illustrate a combination of the two points made by Mr. Thurber and Mr. Soto. The best laid plans of a child unaware of consequences can go awry quite quickly.

To illustrate this point to a general audience, our writer uses the first person point of view to relate a story about his taking his father's car without permission and without a driver's license.

The time is the recent past, and the place is an urban neighborhood. The major sequence of events is as follows:

1. Parents take car to church.
2. Narrator walks to church and takes car.
3. Narrator plans to return car to same spot before the end of the service.
4. Narrator picks up friends.
5. Car runs out of gas.
6. Motorist offers to help but only to take narrator back to the church to meet parents.

We could go on, but you get the idea. The characters are obviously going to be the narrator, his parents, his friends, and the motorist, and, oh yes, the police and the pastor. The primary tension is going to revolve around getting the car back before the narrator's parents leave the church after the service.

Get ready, get set. Go! This is now your practice time. You are going to do the prewriting for your own narrative. If you can't immediately think of a point you'd like to make or a story you'd like to tell, how about an incident that you've either been a part of or witnessed that could be used to illustrate an aspect of being a student, a younger or older sibling, the oldest or youngest child, the only child, parental mishaps, getting even, the joy of winning, brotherhood, friendship, and so forth.

Warm-Up 19

- The point I want to make is _____
  _____
  _____ .

- To illustrate this point, I will tell a story that focuses on _____
  _____
  _____ .

- I will tell this story using the following point of view: ____first person ____third person objective, ____third person omniscient, ____ stream of consciousness

- The major sequence of events: _____
  _____
  _____

- The temporal basis of my story will consist of
  - The time: _____
  - The place: _____

- The characters/people in my narrative will be _____
  _____
  _____ .

- The primary tension will revolve around _____

_____

_____.

Once this information is in place, you can begin to think about the opening that will contain your thesis. Our writer has written the following, which contains the thesis. *I was tremendously angry that Mom and Dad would decide to ruin MY secret plans to accommodate their own needs. I would NOT be denied. Therefore, I schemed, without parental permission and without a driver's license.*

Pick up your pen, or put your fingers on the keyboard. What will you write to introduce your thesis?

- Here's my thesis and the surrounding sentences that will get my narrative up and running. _____

_____

_____

_____

_____

_____

_____

_____

_____.

Checklist

Do your thesis and surrounding sentences

- introduce your audience to the focus of the story?____yes ____no

- give a hint as to the point of the story? ____yes ____no

- make it clear what the point of view is? ____yes ____no

- introduce the setting? ____yes ____no

- introduce the major character(s)? ____yes ____no

- give an indication of the tension in the story? ____yes ____no

If you answered "no" to any of these questions, you need to revise.

- Here's my revised thesis and the surrounding sentences.

_____

_____

_____

_____

_____

_____

_____

_____.

Argument

A writer could use any of the previous rhetorical strategies to construct an argument. **In a very real sense, ALL writing is argument because all writers attempt to have their readers believe and accept the point being made by their presentations.** We argue with ourselves and the world around us countless times each day as we make our ways in life. There are those who draw a fine line between argument and persuasion; wherein, **argument employs logical reasoning** to get the audience to accept the assertion, and **persuasion uses a combination of logic and emotion. For our purposes here, we use the term** *argument* **to cover both argument and persuasion.**

You would construct an argument if you wanted: (1) to express you own assertion, (2) to qualify or oppose another's point of view, or (3) to convince an audience to alter its own stand on an issue. Below are three brief excerpts from longer pieces. Can you identify into which of these three categories each of these selections belongs?

> *In sum, intercollegiate athletics has come to have too pronounced an effect on colleges and universities—and on society—to be treated with benign neglect.*
>
> —James J. Shulman and William G. Bowen,
> *The Game of Life: College Sports and Educational Values*

Shulman and Mr. Bowen are expressing their own opinion about the effect of intercollegiate sports on higher education and society.

> *But if we cannot ourselves hold to the principle that the right to express views must be defended even when the views offend listeners, including ACLU members, we can hardly call on governments to follow that principle.*
>
> —Abba P. Lerner, ACLU's Grievous Mistake,"
> *The New York Times*, 1978

Based on this sentence, we can conclude that Mr. Lerner is qualifying an already existing position of others.

> *Institutions stop teaching and set aside entire weeks for [comprehensive final] tests. Some even give students extra days without classes before exam week to prepare. Legends of all-nighters . . . abound. Clearly, many alumni have fond memories of these academic hell weeks—of having survived and proved themselves. Yet maybe this great tradition is dysfunctional.*
>
> —Karl L. Schilling and Karen Maitland Schilling,
> "Final Exams Discourage True Learning,"
> *Chronicle of Higher Education*, February 2, 1994

In this example, Mr. and Mrs. Schilling are making known to their audience their personal opinion about days being set aside for final exam prep on college campuses.

Recognition time! You should allow yourself some practice time recognizing arguments when you see them—their subjects, points of view and purpose.

1. The easiest thing is to go to your school newspaper and read the editorial page and the letters to the editor. This, alone, will provide more than enough practice material.
2. Want still more? Do the same thing with your local newspaper.
3. During election season, why not take a look at the TV ads of politicians running for office. This is a truly fertile field to harvest.

Once you know your subject, your purpose, and the type of audience you'll be writing for, you can continue with the prewriting routine by deciding on what type of argument you'll construct. Are you going to base it on your own reputation and experience? Will you construct your argument based on logic or reason? Or, do you want to appeal to the emotions of your audience?

Our writer is interested in the "winner takes all" versus the "proportional" forms of representation in government assemblies and parliaments. Based on his own experience, observation, and research, our writer has quite strong feelings about the value, honesty, and viability of proportional representation. He would very much like to defend his own assertion about the two different forms. He is not an expert in either field but has done some in-depth reading and has watched a number of Public Broadcasting specials on the topic. Because of this, he decides against using an argument that is based on his own experience and reputation in this area. Therefore, he must choose between the other two types. Because his audience is a general one and one with myriad opinions and backgrounds, our writer believes an appeal to logic and reason will provide his best argument.

Feel the ideas kick into gear. It's time for you to take a stand. Choose a subject or issue about which you have a strong opinion.

Warm-Up 20

- An issue/subject I have a strong opinion about is _____

  _____

  _____.

- The purpose of my argument will be to____express and defend my own assertion ____qualify or oppose another's point of view____convince my audience to change its mind or behavior.

- My audience is _____.

- I will base my argument on____personal reputation and experience, ____logic and reason, or____emotions of the audience.

That done, the next steps include making a quick list of the following:

1. The reasons why you hold your strong opinion
2. Who would agree with you

3. Who would disagree with you

4. Reasons why they would disagree with you

A most important step involves your taking a careful look at these lists and determining whether you will use the inductive or the deductive approach to the organization of your argument.

> To review quickly, **inductive reasoning** (specific to general) draws conclusions or generalizations based on specific examples/events that are truly representative of the general area being examined. **Deductive reasoning** (general to specific) is developed by presenting specific examples that are drawn from the generalization about the subject.

Our writer has made his list and has chosen to use the deductive approach to organizing his argument. His generalization is that the proportional form of representation is more democratic than the "winner takes all" form. His list of reasons why he holds this opinion, those who agree with him, and those who disagree with him will all provide the possible specifics to support his assertion.

What's your decision? Think about your subject, and complete the following:

Warm-Up 21

- Three major reasons why I hold this opinion are:

  1. _____

  2. _____

  3. _____

- I think the following would agree with me: _____

  _____

  _____

- These people or groups would agree with me because _____

  _____

  _____.

- I believe the following would disagree with me: _____

  _____

  _____

- These people or groups would disagree with me because _____

  _____

  _____.

- I have decided to use the_____deductive approach_____inductive approach.

This preliminary information will provide you with enough material to both compose your thesis statement and write your outline and first draft. For our purposes, we will only write the thesis. Our writer's thesis statement is: ***Polls indicate that most Americans believe that when a politician wins an election, the true voice of the people will be represented in the government. However, true representation of the people's voices lies in proportional representation.*** This is certainly not an emotional statement of our writer's assertion, but it does indicate his strong position regarding representation in government. It also makes it clear that he knows there is a large number of people who would oppose him. Given the generalization made, the reader can expect a **deductive** argument.

Take a deep breath; consider your preliminary information; compose! That's your task at this time. Just as our writer did, you need to think and to write the first draft of your thesis statement.

Warm-Up 22

- Here is my thesis statement: _____

  _____

  _____

  _____

  _____

  _____

Checklist

- My thesis clearly presents the subject and my position._____yes_____no

- My thesis gives a clear indication that my purpose is to_____express my own opinion, _____qualify or oppose another point of view, _____convince my audience to change its mind or behavior.

- My thesis indicates that I will base my argument on_____my own reputation and experience,_____logic and reason,_____emotions of my reader.

- I indicate to my reader that my argument will be_____inductive, _____deductive.

  If you've answered "no" to any of these questions, you need to revise. Rethink and rewrite.

- Here is my revised thesis: _____

  _____

  _____

  _____

  _____

Although you are not going to write a complete argumentative essay at this time, it is very important to review an absolute requirement for a valid argument. **If you want your audience to accept your opinion, you must make certain to avoid logical fallacies.** These errors in reasoning can easily lead your audience to suspect both your assertion and your support for it. Some of the most common logical fallacies are the following:

- **Non sequitur argument:** This Latin phrase means "does not follow." This is the argument that has a conclusion that does not follow from the premise. (Example: Bob drives a Mercedes convertible. He must have a great deal of money and live in a mansion.)

- **Begging the question:** Here is a mistake in which the writer assumes in his assertion/premise/thesis something that really needs to be proved. (Example: All good citizens know the Constitution's Bill of Rights. Therefore, a test on the Bill of Rights should be given to all those registering to vote.)

- **Circular reasoning:** This mistake in logic restates the premise rather than giving a reason for holding that premise. (Example: Science should be required of all students because all students need to know science.)

- **Strawman argument:** Here is a technique we've all seen and heard used by politicians seeking election. The speaker/writer attributes false or exaggerated characteristics or behaviors to the opponent and attacks him on those falsehoods or exaggerations. (Example: You say you are for allowing only people over 21 to vote. I'll never understand why mean, simple-minded activists like you are willing to deny democratic freedoms to millions of citizens.)

- **Ad hominem argument:** This literally means to "argue against the man." This technique attacks the person rather than dealing with the issue under discussion. (Example: We all know that Romulus was forced to leave college. How can we trust his company with our investments.)

- **Hasty generalization:** A person who makes a hasty generalization draws a conclusion about an entire group based on evidence that is too scant or insufficient. (Example: The well-known computer expert found a virus in his own PC. All computers must be contaminated with this virus.)

- **Overgeneralization:** This is what we call stereotyping in most cases. Here, the writer/speaker draws a conclusion about a large number of people, ideas, things, etc., based on very limited evidence. (Example: All members of the Wooden Peg Club are not to be trusted.) Words such as *all, never, always, every,* are usually indicative of overgeneralization. It's best to use and to look for qualifiers (*some, seem, appear, often, perhaps, frequently,* etc.), which indicate that the writer has an awareness of the complexities of the topic or group under discussion.

- **Post hoc argument:** This fallacy cites an unrelated event that occurred earlier as the cause of a current situation. (Example: I had an argument with my best friend the night before my driver's test; therefore, I blame her for my failure.)

- **Either/or argument:** With this fallacy, the writer asserts that there are only two possibilities, when, in reality, there are more. (Example: Tomorrow is my chemistry final; therefore, I must study all night, or I will fail the course.)

Hundreds of books contain instructions on how to construct an argument, and your own AP English instructor will undoubtedly spend some time going over argument and have you write and analyze many samples. But, before leaving this rhetorical strategy, we would recommend that when writing, revising, and analyzing an argument, you check to see if the following are part of the presentation:

> ## A General Checklist for Argumentative Essays
> - A clearly developed thesis is evident.
> - Facts are distinguished from opinions.
> - Opinions are supported and qualified.
> - The speaker develops a logical argument and avoids fallacies in reasoning.
> - Support for facts is tested, reliable, and authoritative.
> - The speaker does not confuse appeals to logic and emotion.
> - Opposing views are represented in a fair and undistorted way.
> - The argument reflects a sense of audience.
> - The argument reflects an identifiable voice and point of view.
> - The piece reflects the image of a speaker with identifiable qualities (honesty, sincerity, authority, intelligence, etc.).

Synthesis

In almost any college course, you will be expected to write essays and make presentations that develop your point of view on a particular subject while incorporating cited, appropriate sources in support and illustration of your position. **This is known as synthesis.** If you've completed a research project in high school, you are probably familiar with the process of locating sources and choosing and citing the ones you will use in your presentation.

Keep in mind that there are two types of synthesis:

- An **explanatory synthesis** is an essay that you've probably constructed many times. In it, you use sources to help your audience understand a particular subject. For example, you research *blood diamonds* and incorporate several sources in your presentation with the goal of having your reader become aware of just what *blood diamonds* are.
- An **argument synthesis** presents your position/point of view, which is debatable, on a topic that is supported by appropriate materials drawn from outside sources. Using the previous example, you might find yourself developing your position that the international ban on *blood diamonds* should continue even though mining these diamonds provides employment in a depressed area of Africa.

Given the nature of the AP English Language exam, it is most likely that you will be presented with a prompt that requires you to write a synthesis essay in the form of an argument. **The synthesis essay requires you to use the skills you've developed in analysis and argumentation.** We strongly urge you to review these skills developed in earlier sections of this chapter.

> ## A General Checklist for Synthesis Essays
> - Establish a position on the issue.
> - Critically read all given texts and any introductory material provided.
> - Annotate your sources.
> - Select appropriate sources to support your position and purpose.
> - Choose appropriate excerpts from each of the selected sources that will help develop the thesis.
> - Summarize, paraphrase, draw inferences from selected material.
> - Make certain you properly cite each source you incorporate into the essay.
> - Construct a conclusion that clearly states a strong, final point.

A General Checklist for Critical Reading of Sources

Critical reading of texts specifically for the synthesis essay is an absolute must. It demands that you determine the following:

- purpose/thesis
- intended audience
- type of source (primary, secondary)
- main points
- historical context
- authority of the author
- how the material is presented
- type of evidence presented
- source of the evidence
- any bias or agenda
- how the text relates to the topic
- support or opposition toward the thesis

Warm-Up 23

Below is a recent court decision on cheerleading as a sport. Carefully read the text and complete the statements that follow.

United States District Court, District of Connecticut
Stephanie Biediger, et al., Plaintiffs v. Quinnipiac University, Defendant

Memorandum of Decision

In March 2009, the defendant Quinnipiac University announced plans to cut three of its sports teams: the women's volleyball team, the men's golf team, and the men's outdoor track team. Contemporaneously, the University pledged to create a new varsity sport, competitive cheerleading, for the 2009–2010 season. Those decisions form the basis of this lawsuit. Plaintiffs Stephanie Biediger, Kayla Lawler, Erin Overdevest, Kristen Corinaldesi, and Logan Riker are five current Quinnipiac women's varsity volleyball players, and plaintiff Robin Lamott Sparks is their coach. Together, they allege that Quinnipiac's decision to eliminate its volleyball team violates Title IX of the Education Amendments of 1972 (20 U.S.C.§ 162, *et seq.*) and the regulations adopted pursuant thereto (34 C.F.R. Part 106) ("Title IX") . . .

Although the plaintiffs allege several theories for relief under Title IX, the parties agreed to sever and try independently the plaintiffs' first claim: that Quinnipiac discriminates on the basis of sex in its allocation of athletic participation opportunities. The parties tried that claim in a bench trial held from June 21 to June 25, 2010. My findings of fact and conclusions of law are set forth herein.

I conclude, as a matter of law that Quinnipiac discriminated on the basis of sex during the 2009–2010 academic year by failing to provide equal athletic participation opportunities for women. Specifically, I hold that the University's competitive cheerleading team does not qualify as a varsity sport for the purposes of Title IX and, therefore, its members may not be counted as athletic participants under the statute. Competitive cheer may, some time in the future, qualify as a sport under Title IX; today, however, the activity is still too underdeveloped and disorganized to be treated as offering genuine varsity athletic participation opportunities for students . . .

Conclusion

I find in favor of the plaintiffs on their first claim for relief in their first amended complaint. A declaratory judgment shall issue that the defendant, Quinnipiac University, has violated Title IX and the regulations promulgated pursuant thereto by failing to provide equal athletic participation opportunities to its female students.

Furthermore, Quinnipiac is hereby enjoined from continuing to discriminate against its female students on the basis of sex by failing to provide equal athletic participation opportunities . . .

IT IS HEREBY ORDERED that, within 60 days, Quinnipiac University shall submit to the court a compliance plan detailing how it will achieve compliance with Title IX and its regulations. That compliance plan shall provide for the continuation of the women's volleyball team during the 2010–2011 season.

It is so ordered.

Dated at Bridgeport, Connecticut, this 21st day of July 2010.
Stefan R. Underhill, United States District Judge

1. Purpose/thesis of the text: _____

2. Intended audience: _____

3. Main points: _____

   _____

4. Historical context: _____

5. Authority of the author: _____

6. Type of evidence: _____

7. Source of evidence: _____

8. Any bias or agenda: _____

9. How text relates to topic: _____

10. Does or does not support thesis: _____

Critical Reading of Visuals Is a Must

As with the steps involved in the critical reading of written material, visuals also require critical analysis. The following are steps you should consider when faced with a visual text:

- Identify the subject of the visual.
- Identify the major components such as characters, visual details, symbols.
- Identify verbal clues such as titles, tag lines, date, author, dialogue.
- Notice position and size of details.
- Does the visual take a positive or negative position toward the issue?
- Identify the primary purpose of the visual.
- Determine how each detail illustrates and/or supports the primary purpose.
- Does the author indicate alternative viewpoints?

Warm-Up 24

Below is a political cartoon related to the recent court decision on cheerleading as a sport. Carefully read the visual and complete the statements that follow.

Cheerleading Athletes
BY PARKER, FLORIDA TODAY

1. Subject of the cartoon: _____

2. Major components: _____

3. Verbal clues: _____

4. Position and size of details: _____

5. Point of view of the cartoonist: _____

6. Primary purpose of the cartoon: _____

7. How details illustrate the primary purpose: _____

_____

_____

8. Indication of alternative viewpoints: _____

_____

Total Workout

If you want to turn the individual warm-up exercises suggested in this chapter into a full out workout, try this: Choose an artifact—something made by humans—and explore it using each of the rhetorical strategies we've just reviewed. With this artifact as your subject, write a series of thesis statements that make assertions about the item, one for each of these strategies.

This is a drawing of the artifact:

Diameter = $1\frac{5}{8}''$ 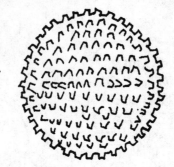   Color = dark green
Weight = 3 oz.   Material = hard rubber

Here are the sample statements using the various rhetorical strategies:

Cause/effect: When I squeeze this little green, rubber ball, my hands tingle.
Classification: This is a green, hard rubber sphere that is used for hand exercise and rehabilitation.
Contrast/comparison: This green rubber ball is smaller than an orange but larger than a golf ball.
Exemplification: This ball was given to me by my personal trainer to strengthen my tennis grip.
Definition: The hand massager is a hard rubber ball with small rubber extensions around the entire sphere used to strengthen hand muscles.
Narration: One day my personal trainer Percival presented me with this perfectly precious green rubber ball.
Process: To get maximum benefit from the hand massager, grip it firmly in the palm of the hand and squeeze and release in 4 sets of 50.
Description: The hand massager is like a round, hard, flattened pinecone.
Argument: Everyone should own and use the hand massager.
Synthesis: I am skeptical about the recent statistics and anecdotes that claim that the hand massager will strengthen hand muscles better than any other device.

In this chapter, we have concentrated your efforts on a review of the rhetorical strategies and the skills connected to prewriting and constructing the thesis statement for a personal essay. We are certain that you will be able to apply these skills to the more complex task of composing a complete personal essay. And, if you can utilize these strategies in a personal essay, you can recognize and analyze them in the writings of others.

CHAPTER > 5

Review the Basics of Rhetorical Analysis

IN THIS CHAPTER

Summary: Learn how to achieve your rhetorical purpose using the tools of analysis

Key Ideas
- ✪ Practice with the most common figures of speech
- ✪ Use the rhetorical question
- ✪ Review rhetorical techniques, including diction, syntax, and attribution
- ✪ Practice with the powers of organization
- ✪ Acquaint yourself with the rhetorical keystone
- ✪ Acquaint yourself with the Rhetorical Triangle Schema

"One of the most difficult things is the first paragraph. . . . Once I get it, the rest just comes out very easily."
—Gabriel García Márquez

This next set of writing warm-up exercises will have you reviewing and working with rhetorical devices and techniques and, then, writing style. In the previous chapter, you flexed those muscles that recognize and develop material according to a specific rhetorical pattern or strategy. **If a rhetorical strategy is the carefully developed plan for achieving a specific writing purpose, then** *rhetorical devices* **are the tools and mechanisms the writer employs to produce that plan, and the rhetorical technique is the manner in which the author uses these tools or devices.**

As an example, let's examine a simple task: draw a square. The equipment includes a straight-edged object, a pencil, and a piece of paper. In writing parlance, to "draw a square" would be the writing purpose, deciding whether to draw it free hand, to use a template, or to trace it would be the rhetorical strategies, and the listed equipment would be the rhetorical devices. These are the tools that enable you to develop that strategy. How the person positions the paper, holds the straight-edged object and places it on the paper, how the person holds the pencil and draws the line would ALL be referred to as rhetorical techniques (in some cases, this is termed *style*).

Rhetorical Devices

Let's begin with rhetorical devices, those writing tools and mechanisms that an author uses to develop a specific strategy. Because this section of the book is concerned with stretching and flexing exercises, we will not be examining all of the possible rhetorical devices. (You may be interested in knowing that there are over 60 of them.) We will have you working out with the most often used and analyzed of the rhetorical devices in an AP freshman college level English course, whether in composition or in literature.

Here is the list of the most used and referred to rhetorical devices and figures of speech that you will be working with during your warm-up activities.

Alliteration	Hyperbole	Parenthesis
Allusion	Metaphor	Personification
Analogy	Metonymy/Synecdoche	Rhetorical Question
Antithesis	Onomatopoeia	Simile
Apostrophe	Oxymoron	Understatement/Litotes
Epithet	Parallelism	

Circle those terms that you know; those you currently can both recognize and use in your own writing. These are the devices you will most probably skip over or just briefly review. For the rest, carefully work your way through each set of exercises. In mostly alphabetical order, we provide a definition, an example, and practice for each of the terms. At the end of this section, there is a self-test that will allow you to evaluate your working knowledge of these particular rhetorical devices.

Alliteration is the repetition of the initial consonant sounds in a group of words. For example, Tommy towed the tiny truck to the town dump. Repeating the "t" sound is an obvious use of alliteration. Now, you try one by filling in the missing letter in the following sentence. The ____ ong, ____ ow ____ incoln ____ urched ahead after the ____ ight turned green. Easy, right? The initial consonant sound being repeated is ____.

Warm-Up Exercises

Warm-Up 1

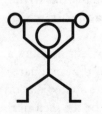

• How about trying an original one on your own? _____

_____

_____.

• The initial consonant used in this sentence is ____.

- Here's an example of alliteration I found in my reading: _____

  _____

- The initial consonant used in this example is ____.

Allusion is an indirect reference to another idea, person, place, event, artwork, etc., to enhance the meaning of the work in which it appears. Allusions can be mythological, biblical, historical, literary, political, or contemporary. The writer assumes that the audience or a specific part of the audience will have knowledge of the item to which he or she refers. For example, if a writer were to refer to his or her subject in these terms: "The killer wore the mark of Cain as he stalked his brother," it is assumed that the reader would be assuming his readers are familiar with the biblical story of Cain and Abel. As you read your favorite periodicals or as you read your class assignments, be aware of allusions and jot down a few as practice and review.

Warm-Up 2

- Here's an example of an allusion that I found in my own reading.
  This is the statement that contains the allusion:

  _____

  _____.

  I found this in _____.

  The allusion is to _____.

- Here is an original allusion I created: _____

  _____

  _____

  The allusion is to _____.

Analogy is comparison between two different items that an author may use to describe, define, explain, etc., by indicating their similarities. Here's an example from Gary Soto's *A Summer Life*. "The asphalt softened, the lawns grew spidery brown, and the dogs crept like shadows." Did you recognize the two analogies? The appearance of the lawns is compared to spiders, and the way dogs walk is compared to shadows.

Can you spot the analogy in the following selection from Norman Mailer's *The Armies of the Night*? ". . . even the pale institutional green paint of the walls would be the same. Perhaps even the prison would not be so dissimilar." Here, _____ is being compared to _____. (If you saw that the walls or the room were being compared to a prison you're right on track.)

You're on your own. Take those periodicals you read regularly; take your class assignments; we're certain you will be able to locate many, many examples of analogy—some using "like" and "as"; others not.

Warm-Up 3

- An example of an analogy I found was in _____

_____.

The statement reads "_____

_____

_____

_____."

In this example, _____ is compared to _____

_____

- Here is an example I created: _____

_____

_____

Antithesis is just that—two opposing ideas presented in a parallel manner. For example, we've all used the expression *Sometimes I love . . . , and sometimes I hate. . . .* Notice the parallel structure of the opposing ideas. There is probably no better example of this device than the opening of Charles Dickens's *A Tale of Two Cities.*

> *It was the best of times, it was the worst of times, it was the age of wisdom, it was the age of foolishness, it was the epoch of belief, it was the epoch of incredulity, it was the season of Light, it was the season of Darkness . . .*

The strength of the parallelism lies with its grammatical structure, "It was the . . . ," where each opposing side is structured with the same pattern.

Can you recognize the antithesis in this statement from Alexander Pope?

> *To err is human, to forgive, divine.*

The parallel structure is created with _____. (If you recognized the use of infinitives, you've got the idea.)

Give it a try. This may not be the easiest rhetorical device to find on a casual basis, but keep your eyes open and your mind alert. You may find examples in speeches that you are reading in your history class, essays in your English class, or ads in your favorite periodicals. They're out there.

Warm-Up 4

- Eureka! I found an example of antithesis. I located it in _____

_____.

The statement is "_____

_____

_____

_____."

The two opposites are _____ and _____.

The parallel structure is created by _____.

Here's my own antithesis: _____

_____

_____.

The two opposites are _____ and _____.

The parallel structure is created by _____.

Apostrophe is a device or figure of speech that is most frequently found in poetry. When a writer employs apostrophe, he or she speaks directly to an abstract person, idea, or ideal. It is used to exhibit strong emotions. Here is an example from Yeats:

> _Be with me Beauty, for the fire is dying._

Can you recognize the direct address to "Beauty" and the strong emotional content of the line? This is apostrophe.

Can you pick out the apostrophe in the following from Shakespeare?

> _Blow, winds, and crack your cheeks._

Simple enough, isn't it? Here the Bard is directly speaking to the "winds" in an imperative appeal.

Try your hand at recognizing apostrophe.

Warm-Up 5

• First, can you spot this figure of speech in the following lines from a Sir Philip Sidney sonnet?

> _With how sad steps, O Moon, thou climb'st the skies!_
> _How silently, and with how wan a face!_

The apostrophe is centered on _____.

The emotion is quite evident with the use of the _____.

(Good for you if you recognized the moon as the apostrophe and the exclamation point as the indicator of emotion.)

• Second, can you find an example of apostrophe in your literature text?

I found an example in _____ by _____.

The line(s) reads "_____

_____."

The apostrophe centers on _____.

The emotional aspect is indicated by _____.

An **epithet** is an adjective or adjective phrase that an author uses to describe the perceived nature of a noun by accentuating one of its dominant characteristics, whether real or metaphorical. Ancient Greece used epithets to characterize their gods and goddesses. For example, in *The Iliad* you can find among the many examples "grey-eyed Athena," "'The wide-ruling king' warned the priest. . . ." Sports figures often acquire epithets, such as "Wilt the Stilt" Chamberlain, "Broadway" Joe Namath, "Mean" Joe Greene, and "Air" Jordan.

Unfortunately, today, epithets are too often used as a weapon for verbal abuse. These abusive phrases can be obscene, sexist, racist, prejudicial, jingoistic, or discriminatory. In this context, Robert Ingersoll said, ". . . epithets are the arguments of malice." When dealing with epithets be aware of their connotative implications.

Can you pick out the epithet in this sentence? *The dark woman smiled at her dark-eyed lover.* (If you recognized that "dark-eyed lover" was an epithet, you've got the idea.)

Step up to the plate. Go to the sports section of your newspaper or a sports magazine and see if you can spot examples of epithets.

Warm-Up 6

- I located an example of an epithet in _____.

Here's the complete statement that contains the epithet.

"_____

_____"

The subject of this epithet is _____.

The actual epithet is _____.

This example treats its subject in a _____ positive _____ negative manner.

So, you've tuned to the TV broadcast of your favorite football team's Sunday afternoon game. The commentators are excited to tell the audience what a *great* game it's going to be, with the two *unbeatable* quarterbacks of these two *super* teams battling it out on their way to winning the *greatest* of sports trophies, the *immortal* coach Lombardi trophy. Zap! You've just been the victim of hyperbole. You know **hyperbole**. This is exaggeration or overstatement to emphasize a point or to achieve a specific effect that can be serious, humorous, sarcastic, or even ironic. The writer needs to be aware of the dangers of overuse, and the reader should be aware that the hyperbolic word or phrase should not be taken literally.

In another example, Robert Burns emphasizes the depth of his love when he says it will last "until all the seas run dry." (That's a lot of loving and a long, long time.) Hyperbole is a mainstay of advertising: the paper towel that is as strong as iron; the kitchen knife that can slice through a silver dollar; the auto sale of a lifetime. We're certain that you can also find hyperbole in song lyrics, ads, and ordinary conversations.

Become an hyperbole detective. Read, look, and listen carefully. We know you are going to discover many examples, one of which you will note below.

Warm-Up 7

- I found this example of hyperbole in/when _____
  _____ .

  Here's the actual hyperbole: _____
  _____
  _____ .

  The hyperbole is emphasizing _____ .

  I think the intended effect is _____ serious, _____ humorous, _____ sarcastic, _____ ironic.

- Here's one I created: _____
  _____
  _____ .

  The hyperbole is emphasizing _____ .

  I want the intended effect to be _____ serious, _____ humorous, _____ sarcastic, _____ironic.

The other side of hyperbole is **understatement**. When a writer wishes to minimize the obvious importance or seriousness of someone or something, he uses understatement, assuming that the audience knows the subject's significance. As with hyperbole, the intended effect of understatement can be serious, humorous, sarcastic, or ironic. In many cases, it indicates politeness, humility, or tact. To hear a firefighter describe the rescue of a family from its fiery home as "*just doing my job*" is an example of understatement. Here the firefighter is being humble about his bravery, and the effect on the audience is ironic.

Be careful. There is a danger that the use or overuse of understatement can be taken as flippant, when that is not the intended effect. If a weather reporter were to comment on a dangerous hurricane as a "little rain shower," she or he might be seen as sarcastic and insensitive.

In presenting an argument, especially to a hostile audience, understatement may prove useful in getting your opinion heard. When writing a letter to the editor opposing the building of a theater next to a school, it may be best to refer to your opponents, not as "hedonistic heathens," but rather as "theater lovers."

One of the most famous examples of understatement is Marc Antony's many references to Brutus and the other conspirators in Shakespeare's *Julius Caesar* as ". . . all honorable men."

Take a stand. You will be able to find examples of understatement in your favorite periodicals and in song lyrics. List one example below.

Warm-Up 8

- I found an example of understatement in _____ .

  The statement reads " _____
  _____
  _____ "

The writer is trying to minimize the _____ importance _____ seriousness of the subject.

I believe the intended effect was to be _____ serious, _____ humorous, _____ sarcastic, _____ ironic. And, I think the understatement was a way to show _____ humility, _____ politeness, _____ tact, _____ none of these.

A special type of understatement is **litotes**. Used for emphasis or affirmation, litotes asserts a point by denying the opposite. For example, *Tornadoes are not unheard of in Nebraska during the summer.* Compare this with *Tornadoes occur frequently in Nebraska during the summer.* (In the first, "not unheard of" is a denial of the opposite of "frequently," which is used in the second sentence.) Litotes can have the same intended effect as any understatement. As another example, compare these two sentences: (1) Our family did not fail to have its usual tension-filled vacation, (2) Our family had a tension-filled vacation. (The first sentence seems more modest in its intent and more sarcastic than the second.)

Can you spot the litotes in the following statement? *Eating that pint of chocolate chip cookie dough ice cream certainly didn't do my diet any good.* (The dieter is affirming the opposite of doing good.)

Now is the time not to give up. (An example of litotes, by the way.) As you read materials for your classes, try your hand at locating an example of litotes.

Warm-Up 9

- I found an example of litotes in _____.

The statement reads "_____

_____

_____"

I believe the intended effect was to be _____ serious, _____ humorous, _____ sarcastic, _____ ironic.

By this time in your educational career, you probably know this next definition by heart. A **metaphor** is a direct comparison between two unlike things, such as "Thine eyes are stars of morning." (Longfellow) In this comparison, *eyes* are compared to morning stars. And, a **simile** is an indirect comparison of two unlike things using *like* or *as*, such as "The short story is like a room to be furnished; the novel is like a warehouse." (Isaac Bashevis Singer). Here short stories are compared to unfurnished rooms and novels to warehouses.

We do this type of comparison all the time. Remember our examination of **analogy.** If you're watching a film in a cold movie theater, you could use a metaphor and say, "This place is a freezer." Or, you could use a simile and say, "This place is like a freezer."

Whether used in poetry or prose, both metaphors and similes engage the imagination of the reader and can make the strange or abstract familiar and concrete. However, it's wise to remember that a little goes a long way—all things in moderation. Also, be wary of:

1. Mixed metaphors/similes, comparisons that do not fit together (I'm such a poor cook that I feel like a bull in a china shop.);

2. Inappropriate metaphors/similes, comparisons that bring up unwanted associations (The popularity of our rock band is spreading like cancer.); and clichés, comparisons that have been overused (That outfit is as old as the hills.).

Remember, a successful writer will always choose material and devices with the purpose and audience in mind.

Now it's time to put on your thinking caps. (Metaphor, if you please.) This should be an easy set of exercises for you. You're going to find examples of metaphors and similes in three different places: in your literature book's poetry section, in your favorite periodical's main article, and in an ad.

Warm-Up 10

- I found a _____ metaphor, _____ simile in the poem "_____" by _____.

  The metaphor/simile is "_____."

  _____ is being compared to _____.

- I found a _____ metaphor, _____ simile in an article titled "_____" that appeared in the _____ issue of _____ magazine.

  The metaphor/simile is "_____."

  _____ is compared to _____.

- I found a _____ metaphor, _____ simile in an ad for _____

  that appeared in the _____ issue of _____ magazine.

  The metaphor/simile is "_____."

  _____ is compared to _____.

Metonymy is another widely used figure of speech. Here is a familiar example. *Today, the White House issued a statement congratulating Congress on its passage of the new energy bill.* You know and we know that the White House did NOT speak, but rather a spokesperson representing the President of the United States. In this case, our close association of the presidency with the White House allows this statement to make sense to us. **Metonymy, therefore, is a metaphor in which the actual subject is represented by an item with which it is closely associated.** Can you identify the metonymic word/phrase in this old adage? *The pen is mightier than the sword.* (If you identified *pen* for words/writing and *sword* for violence/war, you understand what metonymy is.)

Synecdoche is a metaphor that uses a part to represent the whole. Here's a familiar example, *I just got a new set of wheels.* Here the new car is represented by a part of the vehicle, its wheels. Carefully read this example by Joseph Conrad, "Jump, boys, and bear a hand!" It's obvious to the reader that Conrad uses "hand" as a synecdoche to have the speaker exhort his crew to get busy and use their hands and skills to achieve a goal. Can you identify the synecdoche in this phrase: "many moons ago . . ."? (Sure, you recognize that *moons* is being used to represent the passage of months, the cycle of the moon being a part of the monthly passage of time.)

It's important to note that in current literary circles, metonymy is also employed to refer to synecdoche.

Take your mark. Find examples of metonymy and synecdoche in your current class readings and periodicals. By the way, advertising loves these two devices. Pen two samples below. (Metonymy, here.)

Warm-Up 11

- I found an example of metonymy in _____.

  Here's the actual statement. "_____

  _____

  _____."

  The author uses _____ to represent

  _____.

- I also found an example of synecdoche in _____.

  Here's the actual statement. "_____

  _____

  _____."

  The author uses _____ to represent _____.

Beep. Beep. Pow. Zap. Swoosh. We've all seen, read, and heard these words in cartoons, in fiction, in poetry, and on the radio. These are very simple examples of a figure of speech termed **onomatopoeia.** Don't let the word frighten you off. **Onomatopoeia** is simply the word imitating the sound that is being made. Here are some further examples: *buzz, sizzle, lisp, murmur, hiss, roar, splat.* Look carefully at *I quickly swallowed my coffee.* Now, compare it with *I gulped my coffee.* Can you feel the difference between the two? The second sentence uses onomatopoeia to bring you into the scene to actually hear the sound of the speaker drinking and being rushed.

Don't sigh. (Onomatopoeia, here.) Now, it's your turn. Turn to your literature texts and your favorite periodicals to find examples of onomatopoeia. Advertising also makes great use of this figure of speech.

Warm-Up 12

- I found an example of onomatopoeia in _____.

  Here's the statement. "_____

  _____

  _____."

The onomatopoetic word/phrase is "_____."

It is being used to imitate the sound of _____.

Oxymoron is another figure of speech borrowed from the Greek. An **oxymoron** is a paradoxical image created by using two contradictory terms together, such as *bittersweet, jumbo shrimp, pretty ugly*. A writer employs an oxymoron for one or more of the following reasons:

- to produce an effect,
- to indicate the complexity of the subject,
- to emphasis a subject's attributes,
- to be humorous.

Jonathan Swift uses an oxymoron when he states, "I do make humbly bold to present them with a short account . . ." (To be humble and bold at the same time is oxymoronic.) As always, the writer must be aware of his or her purpose and audience and use this device in moderation.

Recognition time. Using your textbooks for English, social studies, and science, look for examples of oxymoron as you read. You will also find them in political speeches, comedy routines, advertising, and song lyrics.

Warm-Up 13

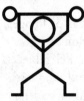

- Hooray! I located one in _____.

Here's the statement that contains the oxymoron. "_____

_____

_____."

The oxymoron is "_____"

I believe that the author's intended purpose is _____ to indicate the complexity of the

subject _____, to emphasize a subject's attributes, _____ to be humorous (ironic, sarcastic,

cynical, witty).

Personification is the final figure of speech we examine. Most of you are familiar with this device. However, for those of you who are not, **personification** is a metaphor that gives human attributes to subjects that are nonhuman, abstract, and/or without life. We've all heard or used the expression, *love is blind*. In this example, love is given the characteristics of a blind person. Personification can be used to describe, explain, define, argue, or narrate. It can also help clarify abstract ideas.

Can you spot the personification in this example from Shakespeare's *Romeo and Juliet?* "Arise fair sun, and kill the envious moon / Who is already sick and pale with grief. . . ." (There are two examples in these two lines. *Sun* is compared to a hunter / killer, while the *moon* is compared to an envious person who is sickly and grieving.) As you can readily see, the use of personification here allows the reader to use his or her imagination much more than with straight reporting.

Warm-Up 14

Give your literary muscles a stretch. (Personification, right?)

- Using only the ads in your favorite periodicals, locate examples of personification. Record one of them below.

  I found an example of personification in an ad for _____.

  The actual line reads "_____."

  In this example _____ is compared to a

  _____.

  My example doesn't have an actual line, but the ad implies that a _____

  is compared to _____.

- Using your literary texts or editorials in your newspaper, locate examples of personification. Record one of them below.

  I found an example of personification in _____.

  The actual line reads "_____."

  In this example _____ is compared to a

  _____.

Parallelism is a rhetorical device used to emphasize a set or series of ideas or images. In **parallel structure**, the writer employs grammatically similar constructions to create a sense of balance that allows the audience to compare and contrast the parallel subjects. These constructions can be words, phrases, clauses, sentences, paragraphs, and whole sections of a longer work. If you go back to our entry for *antithesis,* you will find an excellent example of parallelism in the excerpt from Dickens's *A Tale of Two Cities.* "It was the best of times. . . ." The wide range of antithetical ideas are juxtaposed using parallel structure. The repetition of "It was the" balances all of these opposing thoughts.

In Martin Luther King, Jr.'s "I Have a Dream" speech that he delivered in front of the Lincoln Memorial in 1963, the reader can see the parallelism the audience heard that day. Each major paragraph begins with "I have a dream that. . . ." This parallel structure united and emphasized the equal importance of his main points and helped develop his purpose of exhorting the hundreds of thousands in attendance at this civil rights rally.

Can you identify the parallelism in this statement by Aristotle?

> *For the end of a theoretical science is truth, but the end of a practical science is performance.*

(Right. . . . *the end of a* _____ *is* _____ repeats in both halves of the sentence to emphasize the equal importance of the subjects while remaining different.)

To read, to locate, to record, that is your assignment. (Parallelism using an infinitive, correct?) Okay, grab your textbooks and your periodicals. As you read, keep your eyes open for examples of parallelism. Speeches and writing that try to exhort an audience are good sources.

Warm-Up 15

Record one of your finds below.

- I located an example of parallelism in _____.

  This is the statement that contains parallelism. "_____

  _____

  _____."

  The parallel structure is based on the following construction: _____

  _____.

The **rhetorical question** is the final rhetorical device on our stretching and flexing exercise list. If you pose a question to an audience and do not expect an answer or do not intend to provide one, you have constructed a **rhetorical question**. This device provides a mechanism for the author to get his audience to think about a situation. For example, Ernest Dowson asks, "Where are they now, the days of wine and roses?" One of the more famous rhetorical questions in the world of advertising is "Got milk?" The National Dairy Farmers of America do not expect us to answer that question directly, but they do hope the advertising campaign will encourage the public to both think about milk and buy it.

Can you recognize both the rhetorical question asked by Marcus Aurelius and its purpose? "For if we lose the ability to perceive our faults, what is the good of living on?"

- Do you understand that Aurelius does not intend to either receive a response or to give one to the question?
- Is it clear to you that the author wants to exhort his audience to really think about their faults?"

(If you answered, "yes" to both questions, you have a working knowledge of rhetorical questions.)

You don't want to give up now do you? (That's a rhetorical question alright.) Be aware of the device of rhetorical questions when you read your texts. Often, the writers of textbooks will ask a rhetorical question before beginning a new subject or section. Advertisers frequently turn to the rhetorical question to push their products. Watch for them. Record one of your finds below.

Warm-Up 16

- I located a rhetorical question in _____.

- Here's the actual question. "_____

  _____

  _____."

  The subject of the question is _____.

  The author most probably wants the reader to think about _____

  _____.

Parenthesis is our final term (and, we bet you thought **rhetorical question** was) in this section. This sentence, by the way, contains an example of parenthesis. Take a closer look. **Parenthesis** is a construction (word, phrase, another sentence) that is placed as an unexpected aside in the middle of the rest of the sentence. For example: *If you pick up the kids at 5:00 (by the way, you're a dear for doing this) we can all meet for dinner at the Clubhouse Restaurant.*

Parenthesis can be set off in two ways:

- By parentheses ( ) *The reporter assumed that what the eye-witness said was either true or (at least) closer to the truth than the tale of the accused.*
- By dashes—This tends to be a bit more forceful than parentheses. *The members of the symphonic chorus all said how* great—*Ouch, how I hate that word!*—*the European tour was and how much they learned from their experience.*

For more examples of the dash, consider the excerpt at the end of this chapter.

A writer who decides to employ parenthesis needs to be aware that this intrusion into the middle of the sentence can be a little startling because it is introduced suddenly and is not actually part of the syntax of the rest of the sentence. Parenthesis, with its unexpected "dropping in of the writer," provides the reader with a kind of immediacy and spontaneity. It's almost as if the writer and the reader were involved in a private conversation. The parenthesis can also provide a specific context precisely when it is needed rather than wait for the following sentence or two. For example: *His guitar (he always thought of it as his right arm) was missing again.*

It's now time for you to practice (Oh, no, not again!) recognizing and constructing examples of parenthesis.

Warm-Up 17

- Here's an example of parenthesis that I found: _____
_____
_____
_____
_____.

I located this example in _____.

This example makes use of _____, and the result is to _____

be more conversational _____ provide added information in the immediate

context.

- Here is my own example of parenthesis: _____
_____
_____
_____.

This example makes use of _____, and the result is to _____

be more conversational _____ provide added information in the immediate

context.

Self-Test

Carefully read each of the following statements and identify the rhetorical device/figure of speech contained in each. Some may contain more than one device. You may choose from among these terms:

Alliteration	Hyperbole	Parenthesis
Allusion	Metaphor	Personification
Analogy	Metonymy/Synecdoche	Rhetorical question
Antithesis	Onomatopoeia	Simile
Apostrophe	Oxymoron	Understatement/Litotes
Epithet	Parallelism	

_____ 1. The village went to sleep, window by window. (Edmund Gilligan)

_____ 2. You are as cold and pitiless as your own marble. (Nathaniel Hawthorne)

_____ 3. But if possibility of evil be to exclude good, no good ever can be done. (Samuel Johnson)

_____ 4. Frankly, my dear, I don't feel like dining out.

_____ 5. The true nature of man, his true good, true virtue, and true religion are things which cannot be known separately. (Blaise Pascal)

_____ 6. Clang battleaxe, and crash brand! Let the King reign. (Alfred, Lord Tennyson)

_____ 7. His first irresistible notion was that the whole China Sea had climbed on the bridge. (Joseph Conrad)

_____ 8. Roll on, thou dark blue ocean, roll. (George Gordon, Lord Byron)

_____ 9. He employs over 100 hands on his ranch in Wyoming.

_____ 10. Over the cobbles he clatters and clangs in the dark inn-yard. (Alfred Noyes)

_____ 11. And called for flesh and wine to feed his spears. (Alfred, Lord Tennyson)

_____ 12. Who among you would choose not to attend the rally?

_____ 13. The winner of the Indie 500 told reporters that the win was not his but the result of teamwork.

_____ 14. Sat gray-haired Saturn, quiet as a stone. (John Keats)

_____ 15. The setting sun—red tail-light of the departing day. (Richard Kinney)

_____ 16. The furrow followed free. (Samuel Taylor Coleridge)

_____ 17. Look, he's winding up the watch of his wit; / By and by it will strike. (Shakespeare)

_____ 18. There are millions of people waiting to get through the door.

_____ **19.** Ask not what your country can do for you; ask what you can do for your country. (John F. Kennedy)

_____ **20.** [to Hero,] Thou pure impiety and impious purity . . . (Shakespeare)

(You will find the answers to this self-test in Appendix IV.)

Rhetorical Techniques

KEY IDEA

Now that you've flexed your rhetorical device muscles, you need to move on to the next part of your training routine—**rhetorical techniques**. **Rhetorical techniques** are HOW you use these tools, when, where, how often. It all has to do with choice—choices the writer makes when presenting a particular subject to a specific audience for a specific purpose. These choices revolve around the following:

✓ diction
✓ syntax
✓ tone and attitude
✓ organization

✓ point of view
✓ attribution

Diction

Let's begin this set of exercises with **diction.** You may know **diction** as _word choice_. It's the conscious decision the author makes when choosing vocabulary to create an intended effect. There is almost an infinite number of ways to describe diction. Some of the most often used terms are _formal, informal, poetic, heightened_ (used for special ceremonies and events), _pretentious, slang, colloquial, ordinary, simple, complex,_ etc. A perceptive writer is always aware of the audience, purpose, AND is sensitive to the connotation and denotation of word choice. It makes a difference.

For example, let's suppose you are writing some e-mails or instant messages to several people, including your grandmother, about your birthday celebration.

• How would you describe this event in an instant message to a friend who lives two states away from you?
• How would you describe it in an e-mail to your closest friend from camp?
• And, how would you describe the day's party to your grandmother?

We're betting that your word choice and selection of detail would be quite different in each scenario. Now, you have the idea. It's using the right word in the right place.

Let's look at a situation together. You wake up in the morning with a toothache. You call your dentist and say, "My tooth aches." What kind of pain are you experiencing? Is it sharp, piercing, throbbing, grinding, stabbing, shooting, gnawing, burning, excruciating, agonizing, tortuous, racking, unbearable? Each one of these words has its own denotation and connotation. Do you want to indicate to the dentist that you need immediate relief, even before seeing him or her? Do you want the dentist to see you right away? Is it an emergency? Can it wait? Are you afraid? What is it you want to convey about this toothache? MAKE A CHOICE. Because this toothache is <u>unbearable</u>, you <u>want relief</u> even before you see the dentist. And, because it is an <u>excruciating</u>, <u>stabbing pain</u>, you need to see the dentist <u>ASAP, if not sooner</u>. If you look at the underlined words, it becomes clear that the choices made are indicative of a cry for immediate help. **This is diction.**

As another example, look at the following statements about fog.

1. *Fog forms in the same way as clouds. In fact, fog is a cloud that is on the ground, or with its bottom very near the ground.*
2. *Mists of fog rolled in waves through the tunnels of streets girded with a chain of street lamps.*
3. *The fog comes in on little cat feet.*

• Which one of these statements is atmospheric and almost gloomy? _____

• Which one is not threatening, but rather soft and appealing? _____

• Which one is matter-of-fact, straight to the point, simple? _____

The first statement is straightforward, using ordinary language and is from an encyclopedia entry provided by *USA Today*.com. The second compares fog to surf and includes images of chains and girding. It is not matter of fact, but vivid and edgy. This is from a short story by Isaac Babel titled "Guy de Maupassant." And, the third statement has fog portrayed as a small, gentle cat. This is a line from Carl Sandberg's poem "Fog." Each one of these examples, all with fog as the subject, has a definite effect and purpose. And, that effect is created, and its purpose is developed via diction.

Carefully read each of the following passages.

The skeletal passage:

> *There was a very loud rap song coming from another car. It was so loud the driver could hear every beat and syllable even with his windows rolled up. The lyrics this so-called artist sang were off-color to say the least.*

The fleshed-out passage:

> *A rap song was pounding out of the Camaro with such astounding volume, Roger Too White could hear every single vulgar intonation of it even with the Lexus's windows rolled up.* How'm I spose a love her . . . —*sang or chanted, or recited, or whatever you were supposed to call it, the guttural voice of a rap artist named Doctor Rammer Doc. Doc, if it wasn't utterly ridiculous to call him an artist.* (A Man in Full, *Tom Wolff*)

• Let's consider the diction in the two versions.

Is the subject the same? _____ yes _____ no

Is the sequencing the same? _____

Is the effect the same? _____

(The answer to the first question is yes. For the second question, the answer is for the most part, yes. In answer to the third, definitely not. The effect of the first is one of basic disapproval. The effect of the second is blunt, forceful, and prosecutorial. In the first, there is little specificity and few words to indicate disapproval and how strong it is. However, the second passage has specifics regarding makes of cars, names of characters, and a sample of lyrics. Words and phrases such as "astounding volume," "vulgar intonation," "guttural voice," and "utterly ridiculous" all contribute to the overall effect of searing disapproval. This is the result of diction.)

Syntax

Syntax and **diction** are usually considered together, so we'll continue that tradition. Basically, **syntax** is the grammatical structure of sentences. We do not mean the strict grammatical construction that you learned in the lower grades. We mean the carefully chosen sentence structure and variety a writer uses to develop the subject, purpose, and/or effect. For example, "I read that article last night," and "That article I read last night" use exactly the same words and are equally valid sentences, but the structure and the effect of each is different. This is syntax. To discuss syntax, you should have a working knowledge of each of the terms in the following list of basics.

✓ phrases (*at the same time*)
✓ main clauses (*Horatio watches the* Today *show.*)
✓ subordinate clauses (*before Horatio goes to work*)
✓ declarative sentence (*Horatio watches.*)
✓ imperative sentence (*Horatio must watch.*)
✓ exclamatory sentence (*Horatio really watches!*)
✓ interrogative sentence (*Does Horatio watch the* Today *show?*)
✓ simple sentence (*Horatio watches the* Today *show.*)
✓ compound sentence (*Horatio watches the* Today *show, and he eats his breakfast at the same time.*)
✓ complex sentence (*As Horatio eats his breakfast, he watches the* Today *show.*)
✓ compound–complex sentence (*Before he goes to work, Horatio eats his breakfast, and he watches the* Today *show at the same time.*)
✓ loose sentence (*Horatio watches the* Today *show, and he eats his breakfast at the same time.*)
✓ periodic sentence (*Before going to work and while eating his breakfast, Horatio watches the* Today *show.*)
✓ inverted sentence (*The* Today *show Horatio does watch.*)
✓ paragraphing
✓ punctuation and spelling

If you are not comfortable with any of these items, we suggest, as always, you consult with your English instructor. You may also want to consult the handbook section of an English composition book, Strunk and White's *The Elements of Style,* or one of the Web sites we list in Appendix III.

Wrap your know-how around this exercise. See if you can combine the following short, simple sentences into an example of the specified sentence type.

Warm-Up Exercises

Warm-Up 18

• *The pilot flew the plane. The plane landed smoothly. The plane landed at O'Hare Airport. The passengers were quite happy. The passengers had been on a long trip. The plane landed safely.*

Combine these brief sentences to create the following:

Compound sentence: _____

_____

_____.

Complex sentence: _____

_____

_____.

Compound–complex sentence: _____

_____

_____ .

Periodic sentence: _____

_____

_____ .

(If you would like to check your sentences with the ones we constructed, go to Appendix IV.)

The words an author chooses and how those words are arranged and organized creates the intended meaning and effect. Syntactical patterns heighten the literary experience because they help lead the reader to "get" the emotional and intellectual connotations of the actual text. When presenting ideas to an audience, the writer should consider what will best create the desired meaning and effect. The noted short story writer Isaac Babel said, "No iron spike can pierce a human heart as icily as a period in the right place."

✓ Do you want to sound like a poet? Try unusual or inverted word order. Imitating Robert Frost, a writer could state, "Whose books these belong to I think I know." This is more unusual than the ordinary "I believe I know who owns these books."
✓ Sentence length can also add to the effect. For example, notice the different "feel" you get from the same information presented using two different sentence length patterns.

    1. "I drive. I have a driving problem. The problem is speed. This problem leads to something. It leads to getting tickets. These tickets could lead to suspension of my driver's license. I must slow down. I must control my need to speed."
    2. "I have this need to speed that has led to two speeding tickets over the past year. If I don't slow down, I'm going to end up having my driver's license suspended."

✓ The use of punctuation within sentences is another contributing factor in the development of meaning and effect.
✓ Interruptions inside sentences can have a direct effect on the meaning. (parentheticals, direct address, apostrophes, exclamations, quotations, etc.)
✓ Parallel structure can help create balance and emphasis.
✓ A shift in word order can indicate that an important idea is being presented.

Take a deep breath and practice recognizing diction and syntax and their effects. Carefully read the following passage from Washington Irving's *Rip Van Winkle* and answer the questions that follow.

Warm-Up 19

In a long ramble of the kind on a fine autumnal day, Rip had unconsciously scrambled to one of the highest parts of the Kaatskill Mountains. He was after his favorite sport squirrel shooting, and the still solitudes had echoed and re-echoed with the reports of his gun. Panting and fatigued, he threw himself, late in the afternoon, on a green knoll, covered with mountain herbage, that crowded the brow of a precipice. From an opening between the trees, he could overlook all the lower country for many a mile of

rich woodland. He saw at a distance the lordly Hudson, far, far below him, moving on its silent but majestic course, with the reflection of a purple cloud, or the sail of a lagging bark, here and there sleeping on its glassy bosom, and at last losing itself in the blue highlands.

- This passage contains _____ sentences.

   Sentences _____ and _____ begin with prepositional phrases.

   Sentence _____ begins with a participial phrase.

   Sentences _____ and _____ begin with the subject.

   The two compound sentences are _____ and _____ .

   Sentences _____ and _____ are simple.

   The only complex sentence is _____ .

   There are _____ loose sentences and _____ periodic sentences.

   Based on this information, I can describe these sentences as ____ all similar, ____ varied.

- The main subject of this passage is _____ .

   Its purpose is to ____ inform, ____ amuse, ____ describe, ____ argue.

   The sentences in the passage ____ do, ____ do not contain many descriptive phrases set off by commas.

   The two items given the most coverage in this excerpt are _____ and _____ .

- An example of personification can be found in sentence _____ .

- The diction can be described as: (Check all that apply.)

____ slang	____ poetic	____ ironic
____ ordinary	____ complex	____ witty
____ graceful	____ simple	____ economical
____ artful	____ torrid	____ conversational

- Based on all of the above information, I can conclude that the overall effect of this passage is

____ wicked	____ wise	____ refreshing
____ gritty	____ clever	____ spicy
____ lyrical	____ austere	____ haunting
____ forceful	____ indifference	

   (You can find the answers to these questions in Appendix IV.)

Tone and Attitude

Tone and attitude are the combination of diction, syntax, and rhetorical devices combined to create the specific written work. If you want to discuss an author's perception about a subject and its presentation to an audience, you are involved with **tone** and **attitude.** The concept here may best be understood by thinking of "tone of voice." Consider how many different meanings the word "yes" can have simply by changing your voice or combining it with body language. A writer doesn't have this available; therefore, he or she must use words and structure to do the same thing.

Generally speaking, most writing programs divide tone into three categories:

- **Informal tone** is used in everyday writing and speaking and in informal writing. It includes:

    slang
    colloquialisms
    regional expressions

(Example: We were really ticked off when we missed the train to the city.)

- **Semiformal tone** is what students use in assigned essays for their classes. This includes:

    standard vocabulary
    conventional sentence structure
    few or no contractions

(Example: We were quite annoyed when we missed the train to the city.)

- **Very formal tone** is what you would find in a professional, scholarly journal or a paper presented at an academic conference. In this situation, you might find:

    polysyllabic words
    professional jargon
    complex syntax that you would not use in ordinary conversations or informal writing

(Example: Unable to catch the commuter train into the city because of a series of miscalculations, we found ourselves in a state of annoyance.)

An author's attitude also includes his or her relationship to his audience as well as to his or her subject. When discussing a writer's attitude toward the reader, consider if he is

✓ talking down to the audience as an advisor
✓ talking down to the audience as a satirist
✓ talking to the audience as an equal
✓ talking up to the audience as a subordinate or supplicant.

Tone and attitude can be described in myriad ways. Some of the more frequent descriptors are:

bitter	objective	idyllic
sardonic	naïve	compassionate
sarcastic	joyous	reverent
ironic	whimsical	lugubrious
mocking	wistful	elegiac
scornful	nostalgic	gothic
satiric	humorous	macabre
indifferent	astonished	reflective
scathing	pedantic	maudlin
confidential	didactic	sentimental
factual	inspiring	patriotic
informal	remorseful	admiring
facetious	disdainful	detached

critical	laudatory	angry
resigned	mystified	sad

It is important to note that a combination of two of these describers is sometimes used, such as "That editorial was critical and didactic."

- Create your own review. Carefully read this fictitious movie review and answer the questions that follow.

Warm-Up 20

Little Miss Muffet is a perfunctory sci-fi thriller boasting one or two harrowing and confusing plot turns. Miss Muffet is toyed with, not acted, by Sandi Curls, who is often a jump ahead of her nemesis—though not always of the audience. The problem with Muffet is that it's heavy on plot and lurid teasers but light on character development. Miss Muffet frightens away any and all interested spiders.

The tone of this review is basically ____informal, ____semiformal, ____formal.

Using the list of describers, I would use the following word(s) to characterize the tone of

the review: _____.

These are the words/phrases that help develop this tone. _____

_____

_____

(If you are interested in our answers, you can find them in Appendix IV.)

To really flex and strengthen your tone and attitude muscles, you can apply the activity above to real review of movies, TV shows, theater, recordings, artwork, books, technology, etc. Use your highlighter or pen to underline those words/phrases that create the tone and attitude you perceive. You might want to keep a collection of favorites for review purposes or to share with your classmates. It's good practice.

Another flexing activity you can try is to take a very simple sentence such as "The car came down the street" and create several different kinds of tone by changing the verb and adding different describers (adjectives, adverbs, metaphors, similes).

Organization

How do you organize your clothes closet? It might be even closer to the truth if we asked, "Do you organize your closet?" In any event, would the organization—or lack of it—tell us something about you? We're betting it would. Likewise, how you organize your English notebook can tell a perceptive observer a good deal about your study habits, interests in the field of English, and your willingness to complete assignments.

So, too, with writing. The way an author presents ideas to an audience is termed **organization**. Having practiced with the different rhetorical strategies, you should be familiar with the following organizational patterns that are most often used:

✓ chronological   ✓ contrast/comparison   ✓ specific to general
✓ cause/effect   ✓ least to most important   ✓ most to least important
✓ spatial   ✓ general to specific   ✓ flashback/fast forward

It should be added that readers respond to organizational patterns. They become aware of the way an author perceives the subject and the world around that subject, and, because of this, the purpose, effect, and tone of the piece are further developed.

Point of View

Point of view is a companion technique to organization. You have all had experience identifying it in literary works. **Point of view** is the method the writer uses to narrate the story. They are:

✓ *First person:* The narrator is the main character of the tale. (I played tennis.)
✓ *Third person objective:* The narrator is an uninvolved reporter. (She played tennis.)
✓ *Third person omniscient:* The narrator is an all-knowing onlooker who tells the reader what the character is thinking, gives background information, and provides material unknown to the characters. (She played tennis unaware that a scout from her first-choice college was in the stands.)
✓ *Stream-of-consciousness:* The reader is placed inside the mind of the character and is privy to all his random or spontaneous thoughts. (Virginia Woolf's *To the Lighthouse*)
✓ *Interior monologue:* A type of stream-of-consciousness, it lets the reader in on a character's on-going thoughts, perception, commentary about a particular subject. (i.e., Hamlet's soliloquy: "To be or not to be . . .")

Attribution

If using outside sources in support of your thesis, as a responsible writer you will need to give credit to these sources and place them appropriately within the text of your essay. You could select from among the following techniques.

For our purposes, we will be referring to this excerpt taken from an ABC News broadcast of June 21, 2010, reported by Russell Goodman of the *Associated Press*.

Connecticut Trial to Determine if Cheerleading Is a Sport

Five members of the Quinnipiac University women's volleyball team, and the team's coach, have sued the school for dismantling the team to use the money for a cheerleading squad.

The players argue that cheerleading does not meet federally defined standards for a "sport" under Title IX, the groundbreaking civil rights law that requires schools to allocate resources equally to men's and women's sports teams . . .

"The outcome of this case could have a chilling effect on women's athletics programs if cheerleading is deemed a sport," said Mary Jo Kane, director of the Tucker Center for Girls and Women in Sports at the University of Minnesota and a Title IX expert unaffiliated with the case.

"No one wants to denigrate cheerleading, but should it be considered sport at the expense of legitimate women's competitive team sports? It's a question of equality," Kane said. "How would people react if the school cut a men's sport like baseball or lacrosse and used those funds for a male cheerleading squad?"

The women volleyball players say a men's team would never lose funding in favor of cheerleading and the players are the subjects of sex discrimination.

"The student plaintiffs allege that the defendant's ongoing sex discrimination in the operation of its varsity athletic program violates Title IX of the Education Amendments of 1972," the students said in their lawsuit.

Though Quinnipiac, located in Hamden, CT, and known more for its political polling than its athletics programs and is a private school, it receives some federal funding and is therefore subject to Title IX requirements.

Ways to Provide Attribution

- **Direct Quotation—Full Citation Provided Within the Sentence**

  Example: In an ABC newscast of June 21, 2010, Russell Goodman reported that Mary Jo Kane, director of the Tucker Center for Girls and Women in Sports at the University of Minnesota and a Title IX expert unaffiliated with the case, stated "The outcome of this case could have a chilling effect on women's athletics programs if cheerleading is deemed a sport."

- **Direct Quotation—Citation Placed Outside the Text**

  Example: "The outcome of this case could have a chilling effect on women's athletics programs if cheerleading is deemed a sport," said Mary Jo Kane, director of the Tucker Center for Girls and Women in Sports at the University of Minnesota and a Title IX expert unaffiliated with the case (Goodman, *ABC News*, June 21, 2010).

- **Paraphrase of the Third and Fourth Paragraphs—Citation Placed Outside the Text**

  Example: In a recent interview, Mary Jo Kane, a Title IX expert unconnected to the case, maintains that if cheerleading is ruled to be a legitimate sport, women's collegiate sports programs would be seriously damaged (Goodman, *ABC News*, June 21, 2010).

- **Combination of Direct Quotation and Paraphrase—Citation Provided Outside the Text** (Note the use of the ellipsis.)

  Example: In a recent ABC news broadcast, Mary Jo Kane, a Title IX expert unconnected to the case, maintains that if cheerleading is ruled to be a legitimate sport, women's collegiate sports programs would be seriously damaged. Kane, director of the Tucker Center for Girls and Women in Sports at the University of Minnesota, stated, "It's a question of equality. How would people react if the school cut a men's sport like baseball or lacrosse and used those funds for a male cheerleading squad?" (Goodman, *ABC News*, June 21, 2010)

Warm-Up 21

Using the cheerleading report above, construct an example of each of the following types of citations. Use different quotations than the ones used above in the examples.

- Direct Quotation—Citation Provided Within the Text

  _____

  _____

  _____

- Direct Quotation—Citation Provided Outside the Sentence

  _____

  _____

  _____

- Paraphrase the Third and Fourth Paragraphs—Citation Provided Outside the Text

_____

_____

_____

- Combination of Direct Quotation and Paraphrase—Citation Provided Outside the Text

_____

_____

_____

Style

When you talk about a writer's choices and the pattern of these choices you are in the world of literary style.

"It's not my style." "Have you seen the style section of the newspaper?" "She dresses with such style." "What style house is that?" "I love standup comedy, but I don't really like the slap-stick style of comedy." Sound familiar? We use or hear or see the word *style* almost everyday. But, if you were to ask someone to define style, chances are that person would have a difficult time putting it into words. So, we'll do it for you. **Style is the unique way an author consistently presents ideas. An author's choice of diction, syntax, imagery, rhetorical devices, structure, and content all contribute to a particular style.** It's an author's writing pattern, if you will. Writing style can vary from author to author, subject to subject, period to period, and even among the same author's different works.

If you were given an empty room and asked to make it your own, what would you do with it? What would you use the room for? What color would you paint the walls? What would be your major piece of furniture? What would be your other pieces of furniture and accessories? How would you light the room? What would you put on the walls and the windows?

You get the idea. Once the room is finished to your specifications, it is yours; it is your style. Thinking about and discussing writing style is very similar to the above process. Any writer comes to the blank page with an idea and purpose in mind. The writer's style is the result of all the decisions made about **how** to present that idea to achieve that purpose.

This is true whether you are examining your own writing style or that of a professional writer. Before going any further, here is a list of those items that literary analysts consider when looking at style:

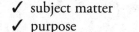

- ✓ subject matter
- ✓ purpose
- ✓ organization
- ✓ point of view
- ✓ diction
- ✓ syntax
- ✓ rhetorical devices and figures of speech
- ✓ attitude
- ✓ tone

You're already familiar with the flexing and stretching exercises for these items. So, as this part of the chapter progresses, you will be examining and practicing how to use them when discussing writing style.

Your first style exercise may be difficult, but don't refuse to do it.

This exercise is about YOUR writing style. If you come across a term that you are unfamiliar or uncomfortable with, check the index of this book or the handbook section of your writing textbook, or ask your AP English instructor. One of these sources is bound to clear things up for you.

Warm-Up 22

- Take one of your essays from your portfolio and complete the following inventory.

My subject is _____.

I use the following mode of discourse: _____.

The primary rhetorical strategy I use to develop my subject is _____

_____.

My purpose is _____.

My audience is _____.

The essay has _____ paragraphs.

Total number of
  sentences = _____

Simple sentences = _____

Compound sentences = _____

Complex sentences = _____

Compound–complex
  sentences = _____

Sentences beginning with
  I/She/He/It = _____

Sentences beginning with A or
  The = _____

Sentences beginning with a
  subordinate clause = _____

Sentences beginning with
  a participial phrase = _____

Sentences beginning with
  a gerund = _____

Sentences beginning with
an infinitive phrase = _____

I use a lot of:

simple, monosyllabic words. _____ yes _____ no

complicated, polysyllabic words. _____ yes _____ no

jargon and/or clichés. _____ yes_____ no

passive voice. _____ yes _____ no

My essay contains the following rhetorical devices: (Check the devices you find times the number of times you use that device in this essay. For example: × analogy × *3*)

_____ parallelism × _____   _____ hyperbole × _____

_____ rhetorical question   _____ understatement

× _____   × _____

_____ analogy × _____   _____ antithesis × _____

The essay also has the following figures of speech: (identify, plus times used; for example: × simile × 7)

_____ alliteration × _____   _____ allusion × _____

_____ apostrophe × _____   _____ metonymy × _____

_____ epithet × _____   _____ metaphor × _____

_____ onomatopoeia × _____   _____ oxymoron × _____

_____ personification × _____   _____ simile × _____

I've read over my complete essay, and I like the following sentence(s) the most. _____

_____

_____

_____

_____

Now, here is a difficult question. Why do you like this sentence? Be honest. No one will see this if you don't want them to. _____

_____

_____

If you had to describe or categorize your own writing, what would you choose from the list below? (Circle all that apply.)

formal	informal	simple	reader-friendly	earnest
simple	complicated	austere	authentic	dreary
effective	interesting	fluent	focused	talky
artful	eloquent	wise	substantive	self-indulgent
distinctive	memorable	strong	revealing	melodramatic
blunt	haunting	compelling	enlightening	elitist
economical	elegant	balanced	thorough	affected
edgy	fresh	bold	contrived	opinionated
dramatic	imaginative	surprising	hyperbolic	abrasive
striking	impassioned	forceful	overdone	flippant
honest	insightful	gutsy	forced	idiosyncratic
dense	gritty	ironic	obvious	insubstantial
paradoxical	funny	witty	formulaic	underdone
amusing	entertaining	delightful	unconvincing	forgettable
offbeat	endearing	refreshing	gimmicky	lackluster
outrageous	spicy	subtle	ordinary	anemic
graceful	serious	provocative	trite	narrow
urbane	thoughtful	sarcastic	lurid	pedestrian
profound	intimate	ironic	shallow	labored

sensuous	down-to-earth	morbid	moralizing	thought-provoking
lyrical	lush	dreamy	sophomoric	awkward
rambling	rhapsodic	sympathetic	simplistic	hackneyed
corny	repetitive	sentimental	maudlin	purple
preachy	abstract	cerebral	pedantic	stiff
pompous	lofty	bookish	wordy	grandiose
pejorative	pretentious	tiresome	grim	nasty
			uneven	predictable

Quite a list isn't it? Actually, this is only about one-third of the descriptors we've seen used to discuss literary style. Don't panic. We are not going to have you working out with each of these terms. However, this list is a handy one to have when you begin to think and talk about your writing style or that of another.

To return to your writing style. If you completed the above activities, you have a pretty good idea about how you write in one, specific instance. If you continue to employ these same tactics in most of your other writing, you could say you have a definite style.

You would use this same process if you wanted to examine the writing style of a particular writer. For example, many English instructors, literary critics, and general readers characterize the writing of Ernest Hemingway as having:

✓ simple grammar
✓ realistic dialogue
✓ accessible diction
✓ austere word choice
✓ blunt descriptions
✓ short, declarative sentences

As another example, when describing the writing style of Isaac Babel, one writer described Babel's style as exhibiting:

✓ economy of words
✓ construction of images from unusual pairings
✓ juxtaposing disparate items.

This writer sees Babel's style as tightly tied to the mood of the narrator, his sense of self-hood, his family, the history of his people, and the political situation in which he finds himself. Finally, Isaac Babel's style is characterized as "lush without being over the top." With practice, you, too, should be able to examine a writer's work and to describe and characterize the literary style.

Total Workout

No pain, no gain. Here's the final exercise for this chapter.

- Carefully read the passage below, excerpted from Edgar Allan Poe's "The Tell-Tale Heart," and answer the questions that follow.

> *True!—nervous—very, very dreadfully nervous I had been and am; but why will you say that I am mad? The disease had sharpened my senses—not destroyed—not dulled them. Above all was the sense of hearing acute. I heard all things in the heaven and in the earth. I heard many things in hell. How, then, am I mad? Harken! And observe how healthily—how calmly I can tell you the whole story.*
>
> *It is impossible to say how first the idea entered my brain; but once conceived, it haunted me day and night. Object there was none. Passion there was none. I loved*

the old man. He had never wronged me. He had never given me insult. For his gold I had no desire. I think it was his eye! Yes, it was this! He had the eye of a vulture—a pale blue eye, with a film over it. Whenever it fell upon me, my blood ran cold; and so by degrees—very gradually—I made up my mind to take the life of the old man, and thus rid myself of the eye forever. Now, this is the point. You fancy me mad. Madmen know nothing. But you should have seen how wisely I proceeded—with what caution—with what foresight—with what dissimulation I went to work! And every night, about midnight, I turned the latch of his door and opened it—oh so gently! And then, when I had made an opening sufficient for my head, I put in a dark lantern, all closed, closed, that no light shone out, and then I thrust in my head. Oh, you would have laughed to see how cunningly I thrust it in! I moved slowly—very, very slowly, so that I might not disturb the old man's sleep. It took me an hour to place my whole head within the opening so far that I could see him as he lay upon his bed. Ha! Would a madman have been so wise as this? And then, when my head was well in the room, I undid the lantern cautiously—oh, so cautiously—cautiously (for the hinges creaked)— I undid it just so much that a single thin ray fell upon the vulture eye. And this I did for seven long nights—every night just at midnight—but I found the eye always closed; and so it was impossible to do the work; for it was not the old man who vexed me, but his Evil Eye. And every morning, when the day broke, I went boldly into the chamber, and spoke courageously to him, calling him by name in a hearty tone, and inquiring how he has passed the night. So you see he would have been a very profound old man, indeed, to suspect that every night, just at twelve, I looked in upon him while he slept.

1. The subject of this passage is _____.

2. The purpose of this passage is to _____ inform, _____ describe, _____ entertain, _____ argue.

3. The passage is told from which point of view? _____ first, _____ third objective, _____ third omniscient, _____ stream-of-consciousness, _____ interior monologue

4. Which two punctuation marks, not used often by most writers, does this author use quite frequently? _____ and _____ (Note: There are three uses for dashes: (1) indicating sudden change, (2) making parenthetical or explanatory material stand out, and (3) summarizing preceding material.)

5. The author uses the dash to _____
_____.

6. An exclamation point is used to indicate sudden or strong emotions. The author of this excerpt employs the exclamation point to indicate _____ sudden, _____ strong emotions.

7. With your answer to question 6 in mind, why can the use of the exclamation point after "—oh so gently" be termed ironic? _____
_____

8. In the phrase "—oh, so cautiously—cautiously (for the hinges creaked)," why would the author use the actual ( ) rather than more dashes? _____
_____

9. To which two senses does this passage focus its attention? _____ and _____

10. Check the rhetorical devices found in this excerpt.

   _____ alliteration   _____ allusion   _____ apostrophe
   _____ analogy   _____ antithesis   _____ litotes
   _____ metaphor   _____ metonymy   _____ onomatopoeia
   _____ oxymoron   _____ parallelism   _____ personification
   _____ rhetorical question   _____ simile

11. Does this passage use punctuation that contributes to the development of the meaning and effect? _____ yes _____ no

12. Does the passage use interrupters that contribute to the development of the meaning and effect? _____ yes _____ no

13. The sentences in this excerpt are _____ all similar _____ varied.

14. The passage _____ does _____ does not contain many descriptive phrases.

15. Which words does the author repeat frequently in this passage?

   _____

16. The diction can be described as (check those that apply)

   _____ economical   _____ ordinary   _____ ironic
   _____ simple   _____ complex   _____ witty
   _____ conversational

17. Based on all of the above information, I can conclude that the overall effect of this passage is (check those that apply)

   _____ chilling   _____ indifferent   _____ lyrical
   _____ suspenseful   _____ torrid   _____ austere

18. Based on my close reading of this passage, I can describe the author's style as (check those that apply):

   _____ anemic   _____ abstract   _____ simple
   _____ hyperbolic _____ ordinary   _____ flippant
   _____ frivolous   _____ dramatic   _____ spare
   _____ sensuous   _____ compelling   _____ complex

19. The excerpt at the beginning of this workout is from pages 3 to 4 of the "Tell-Tale Heart" by Edgar Allan Poe. The short story is included in *Tell-Tale Heart and Other Writings* by Edgar Allan Poe, published in 1983 by Bantam Books, New York, NY. If you were writing an essay about creating tension and suspense in a narrative, how would you provide an appropriate citation for this particular excerpt from "The Tell-Tale Heart"? Check those that correctly apply.

   _____ . . . can be analyzed in Poe's short story (*Writing the AP English Essay*, p. 90).
   _____ In the 1983 Bantam Classics edition of *The Tell-Tale Heart and Other Stories*, Poe begins to establish in the first paragraph of the short story "The Tell-Tale Heart" . . .
   _____ . . . the pacing begins to build (Poe, pp. 2–3).

(You can find the answers to these questions in Appendix IV.)

Your warm-up exercises are now completed. You have reviewed and practiced with the basics of **modes of discourse** in Chapter 3, **rhetorical strategies** in Chapter 4, and **rhetorical devices and techniques,** and the elements of **literary style** in this chapter. You are now ready to step up to a full-fledged writing routine. It is important to keep in mind that you can always return to these warm-up activities and flex those writing muscles that can become stiff and flabby if not used regularly.

Your Rhetorical Keystone

MODES OF DISCOURSE (method a writer uses to have a conversation with a particular reader/audience)

Argument   Description   Exposition   Narration

RHETORICAL STRATEGIES (plan for achieving a specific writing purpose)

Argument   Cause/effect   Contrast/comparison   Definition synthesis

Description   Division/classification   Example   Narration   Process analysis

RHETORICAL DEVICES (tools and mechanisms the writer employs to develop the strategy)

The most used and referred to rhetorical devices and figures of speech include:

Alliteration	Hyperbole	Parallelism
Allusion	Metaphor	Personification
Analogy	Metonymy/synecdoche	Rhetorical question
Antithesis	Onomatopoeia	Simile
Apostrophe	Oxymoron	Understatement/litotes
Epithet	Parenthesis	

RHETORICAL TECHNIQUES (how the author uses rhetorical devices)

These choices revolve around the following:

Attribution   Diction   Organization   Point of view   Syntax   Tone/attitude

Rhetorical Triangle Schema

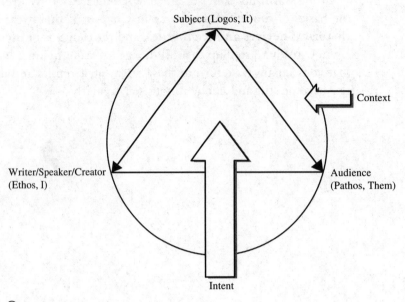

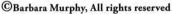

This diagram is an enhanced look at Aristotle's classical rhetorical triangle. All writers must be aware of three focus points: 1) **the subject** – what are you going to write about? 2) **the audience** – for whom are you writing? 3) **YOU, the writer,** how you going to engage this audience?

BUT, not only must the writer address these three focal points, she must be fully aware of **WHY** (**intent**) she is presenting this writing and the **SITUATION (context)** in which this writing is being presented.

Develop Strategies for Success

CHAPTER 6

Reading and Working Different Types of AP English Prompts

IN THIS CHAPTER

Summary: Clarify the expectations of the AP English essays with regard to analysis and argumentation

Key Ideas
✪ Review the specific vocabulary related to the AP English essay prompts
✪ Practice deconstructing AP English essay prompts

"Do not open the mouth until the brain is in gear." (A.A.)

The same also could be said for those preparing to write an AP English essay. **Do not write your AP English essay until your brain is in gear.** Getting your brain in gear starts with deconstructing the prompt.

Continuing with our personal training metaphor, if you have a personal physical trainer, he or she has carefully prepared a specific routine that tells you what to do when you go to the gym for your workout. It clearly states the exercise, the number of repetitions, and the number of sets. To ignore these instructions is to place your physical well-being in jeopardy. The same principle holds true for addressing the AP English essay prompt. It doesn't matter if it's a prompt for a Literature essay or for a Language essay; each assumes that you will read both the prompt and the given text carefully. **The expectation is that you will recognize and pay attention to key terms. Not only are you to recognize these important words, but you are also to have a working familiarity with them. These are the keys to planning and writing your AP English essay.**

Key Words and Phrases

If you are like most of our students, your first question will probably be, "Okay, but just what are these key words or phrases?" **The "key words and phrases" are all related to the two general purposes emphasized by both AP English courses: analysis and argumentation, and they are examined in Chapters 2, 3, and 4 of this book.** If you have skipped any of these sections, you should go back and make certain you are familiar with the material covered in each of these three chapters. For a really quick review, go to the chart at the end of Chapter 4.

Throughout this chapter, and the ones to follow in this section of the book, we not only give you formats, ideas, activities, and thought-provoking questions to consider, but we also model the process for you with actual student samples and commentary on them.

What Constitutes an AP English Prompt?

Remember, a prompt is just that, a suggestion, or hint, or timely instruction as to what is expected of you as a writer in a specific circumstance. As we have said before, the two major writing tasks that AP English courses are preparing for are: (1) analysis of text, and (2) argumentation. Therefore, AP English essay prompts are aimed at developing and evaluating your skills in writing the essay of analysis or a clearly presented and supported argument.

Generally, you could say that the AP English prompt is made up of THREE parts:

Subject + Verb + Object. Sound familiar? You're right; it looks like the basic components of a sentence. And, if you keep this idea in mind, you'll not easily forget to look for each of these three parts when you begin to deconstruct any given prompt.

- **The Subject refers to the given text on which both the prompt and your essay are based.** For example:

  _____ Read the following passage from . . .
  _____ In her book, the author makes the following observation about . . .
  _____ In the following passage, the speaker discusses . . .
  _____ Read the following poem . . .
  _____ Read the following short story . . .
  _____ Writers often highlight . . .
  _____ The author wrote . . .
  _____ Read the following texts relating to a given topic . . .

- **The Verb specifically tells you what to do with the given text.** For example:

  _____ Analyze the rhetorical techniques or strategies . . .
  _____ Defend, challenge, or qualify the writer's ideas . . .
  _____ Analyze how the poet uses imagery . . .
  _____ Analyze how the author uses literary techniques or devices . . .
  _____ Choose a literary work and show how . . .
  _____ Discuss the poem's controlling metaphor . . .
  _____ Explain how . . .
  _____ Other verbs that could be used include: compare, contrast, evaluate, explain, justify, relate, describe, identify and discuss, identify and explain.
  _____ Take a position . . .

- The **Object** is the **goal**. It makes it clear what the overall purpose of your essay is to be. For example:

> _____ . . . Two conflicts within one character illuminating the meaning
> _____ . . . Reveals the speaker's response to . . .
> _____ . . . Author's rhetorical purpose in the passage as a whole . . .
> _____ . . . Author's exploration of . . .
> _____ . . . Expression of the attitude of the speaker . . .
> _____ . . . Revelation of character . . .
> _____ . . . Retelling of an experience . . .
> _____ . . . Support your position by synthesizing at least three of the given sources . . .

A fourth component of an AP prompt that _must_ be considered is the recognition of **key words** and **phrases**. These are clues that let you know what the creator of the prompt is looking for in the organization and structure of your presentation. For example:

- Consider such **stylistic devices** as: diction, imagery, syntax, pacing, structure, tone and selection of detail.
- Using your own knowledge and experiences or readings . . .
- Choose a **suitable** literary work . . .
- Choose a work of literary **merit** . . .
- Consider **formal elements** such as structure, syntax, diction and imagery . . .
- Consider **literary elements** such as point of view, selection of detail, figurative language . . .
- Consider such **poetic elements** as imagery, metaphor, rhythm, form and rhyme . . .

A fifth and final component that many prompts contain is the **inclusion of incidental data**. These are remarks that are made about the given text that can often prove to be quite helpful in both your understanding and analysis of the text. Pay attention to such information as titles, author's name, date of publication, the genre of the text, and any other background that the test maker provides. If the information is given to you, it must be important in your consideration of the text and the preparation of your essay. When synthesizing sources, make sure to provide adequate and appropriate attribution.

> When a prompt reads "such as," you can choose from among the ideas presented, or you can choose to develop your own ideas, strategies and devices. But, be aware that you _must_ adhere to the requirements dictated by the prompt. If it asks for more than one item, you cannot develop only one. No matter how well you develop this one idea, it will fall short of the basic requirements of the prompt.

Once you know what is expected, you will be able to

- Read in a more directed manner;
- Be sensitive to those details that will apply;
- Write an essay that adheres to the given topic.

Workout 1

The following are two AP English prompts from past exams. Using your "prompt deconstructing" knowledge, carefully read and notate each prompt and answer the questions that follow.

A. In the following passage from a letter to her daughter, Lady Wortley Montague (1689–1762) discusses the education of her daughter. Read the passage carefully. Then write an essay in which you analyze how Lady Montague uses rhetorical strategies and stylistic devices to convey her views about the role of knowledge played in the lives of women of her time. (AP Language, 1996)

1. Highlight the subject of the prompt.

2. Underline the key verb(s) of the prompt.

3. Bracket the object/goal of the prompt.

4. The topic of the letter is _____.

5. The letter is one that is written from a _____ to her _____.

6. The historical context is the _____ fifteenth to sixteenth, _____ sixteenth to seventeenth, _____ seventeenth to eighteenth centuries.

7. Will the time period play a necessary role in how the writer addresses the text?

_____ yes _____ no

8. Can the writer choose to address ONLY rhetorical strategies? _____ yes _____ no

9. Can the writer choose to compose an essay about his/her views concerning knowledge and education? _____ yes _____ no

Check your responses with ours. The subject of the prompt is clearly Lady Montague's letter to her daughter, and the key verb is **analyze**. The object/goal of this analysis is the use of rhetorical strategies and stylistic devices. The topic of the letter written from a mother to her daughter is the education of young women. The historical context of the seventeenth and eighteenth centuries would have no real bearing on how the writer addresses the analysis of the text. The prompt makes it clear that the writer must address BOTH rhetorical strategies and stylistic devices. Because this is an essay of analysis, the writer DOES NOT discuss his or her personal views about knowledge and education.

B. Carefully read the following passage from George Eliot's novel *Middlemarch* (1871). Then write an essay in which you characterize the narrator's attitude toward Dorothea Brooke and analyze the literary techniques used to convey the attitude. Support your analysis with specific references to the passage. (AP Literature, 1998)

1. Highlight the **subject** of the prompt.

2. Underline the **key verb(s)** of the prompt.

3. Bracket the **object/goal** of the prompt.

4. For this prompt, is it important to pay close attention to the time period of the novel's setting? _____ yes _____ no

5. Is the writer expected to address all of the possible literary techniques in this passage?

_____ yes _____ no

6. Based on the demands of the prompt, can the essay be an abstract discussion?

_____ yes _____ no

7. Based on the demands of the prompt, can the writer discuss his or her own attitude toward Dorothea? _____ yes _____ no

Compare your responses with ours. The subject of this prompt is George Eliot's novel _Middlemarch,_ and the key verbs are **characterize** and **analyze**. The narrator's attitude toward Dorothea Brooke and the literary techniques used to convey the attitude are the two objects/goals of the key verbs. Even though the date of the novel is provided, it is not important to the type of analysis demanded by the prompt. If the test makers wanted the writer to address all of the possible literary techniques used in the passage, they would have specified ALL. Based on a careful reading and deconstruction of the prompt, the writer should be able to clearly see that an abstract discussion will NOT meet the basic requirements, and neither will a discussion of the writer's personal attitude toward Dorothea.

Workout 2

Carefully read and notate each of the following prompts and answer the questions that follow.

A. The following passage is in the introduction to Martin Luther King, Jr.'s _Why We Can't Wait,_ a book that describes the social conditions and the attitudes of many black Americans in the 1960s. After reading the passage carefully, write an essay that describes the rhetorical purpose of the passage and analyzes its stylistic, narrative, and persuasive devices. (AP Language, 1989)

1. Highlight the **subject** of the prompt.

2. Underline the **key verb(s)** of the prompt.

3. Bracket the **object/goal** of the prompt.

4. The historical context is _____.

5. The writer needs to recognize the author's _____.

6. The two key verbs in this prompt are _____ and _____.

7. The three devices that must be addressed are _____,
_____, and _____.

8. Does the prompt allow the writer to choose from among these three devices?

_____ yes _____ no

B. Read the following two poems carefully, noting that the second includes an allusion to the first. Then write a well-organized essay in which you discuss their similarities and differences. In your essay, be sure to consider both theme and style. (AP Literature, 1988)

1. Highlight the **subject** of the prompt.

2. Underline the **key verb(s)** of the prompt.

3. Bracket the **object/goal** of the prompt.

4. The primary strategy demanded for your essay is ____ cause/effect, ____ argument, ____ contrast/comparison, ____ description, ____ narration.

5. The major clue given to the writer in this prompt is that poem no.2 contains an _____ to poem no.1.

6. Can the writer choose to write about only theme or only style? ____ yes ____ no

(You can find the answers to these questions in Appendix IV.)

Workout 3

As we progress through the book, we will begin addressing two specific essay prompts, one for Language and one for Literature. For each, we deconstruct the prompt, notate the text, plan the essay, and write each section of the presentation. In many situations, we will be using actual student-written material.

Let us introduce you to our two sample prompts.

English Language and Composition

In "A Presidential Candidate," Mark Twain makes his own "modest proposal." Carefully read the text and identify the author's purpose. Then write a well-organized essay in which you analyze Twain's use of rhetorical devices and strategies to achieve his purpose and create humor. You may wish to consider such items as diction, selection of detail, irony, and tone.

Here's what a deconstruction of this prompt would look like:

English Language and Composition

In "A Presidential Candidate," Mark Twain makes his own "modest proposal." Carefully read the text and **identify** the author's purpose. Then write a well-organized essay in which you **analyze** Twain's [use of rhetorical devices and strategies to achieve his purpose and create humor.] You may wish to consider such items as diction, selection of detail, irony, and tone.

---

1. The **subject** is Mark Twain's "A Presidential Candidate."
2. The **key verbs** are identify, analyze.
3. The **object/goal** is the purpose and humor and how it is achieved and created.
4. As I read the text, I will pay **close attention** to diction, selection of detail, irony, and tone, although I could have chosen others.

English Literature and Composition

In "Dover Beach," Matthew Arnold presents an argument for fidelity and love. In a well-developed essay, discuss the techniques Arnold employs to develop his persuasive poem. Refer to such tools of the poet's craft as diction, organization, meter, poetic devices, and imagery.

Here's what a deconstruction of this prompt would look like.

English Literature and Composition

In "Dover Beach," Matthew Arnold presents an argument for fidelity and love. In a well-developed essay **discuss** the [techniques Arnold employs to develop his persuasive poem.] Refer to such tools of the poet's craft as diction, organization, meter, poetic devices, and imagery.

---

1. The **subject** of this prompt is Matthew Arnold's "Dover Beach."
2. The **key verb** is discussed.
3. The **object/goal** is the development of the argument.
4. As I read the poem, I want to pay **close attention** to poetic form, imagery, figurative language, and rhetorical strategies, or others.

After the careful reading and deconstruction of the prompt, the writer is now ready to move on to the prewriting and planning of the essay.

CHAPTER 7

Prewriting and Planning

IN THIS CHAPTER

Summary: Practice with the preliminary steps in the development of your AP English essay

Key Ideas

✪ Generate the raw material of your essay

✪ Notate related texts

✪ Deconstruct accompanying texts on which the AP English Language and Literature prompts are based

---

"A good essay is like a sharpened pencil. It has a point." (A.A.)

You can sharpen that pencil using a mechanical or electric sharpener or just a plain, old penknife. (By the way, the word *penknife* got its name from the small knife that was used to sharpen the ends of quills that would be used as pens.)

Just as a sharpened point of a pencil will produce a fine, clear line, your sharpened writing skills will allow you to present your ideas in a clear and compelling AP English essay. This chapter will provide you with information and practice exercises that will both develop and strengthen your prewriting and planning skills. As your writing trainers, we lead you through the actual process of reading, notating, and organizing your thoughts and materials for an AP English essay.

Prewriting

Prewriting is the process that generates the raw material on which you will base your essay. It can be a messy piece of business, but this messiness can lead to a well-developed

and appealingly designed presentation. From your many years of experience as an English student, you are probably familiar with the prewriting process. This includes:

General Annotating: (See sample prompts and texts)

- Highlighting
- Underlining
- Bracketing

Within the prompt: (See sample prompts)

- Determining the subject
- Deciding on a strategy

Within the text and outside of text: (See sample texts)

• Writing margin notes:	Jot down questions, responses, identifications, etc., in the margins.
• Concept Mapping and Concept Wheels	Group related ideas, examples, points, etc., around a major point. Use circles, squares, and lines to connect specifics to the topic or major point.
• Charting	List ideas, examples, etc., under major headings.
• Questioning	Identify who, what, when, where, why, and how. This technique works quite well for informative and explanatory essays.
• Free Writing	For a set period of time (such as 5-10 minutes), jot down anything about your subject that comes to mind. The important thing is not to stop for the entire time period. This is a good mind-juggling technique for those essay assignments that do not involve timed writing. It's not particularly useful for an essay exam situation.
• Brainstorming	This is a good group pre-writing activity in which the people in the group try to come up with as many possible words or phrases or ideas that can be associated with a given subject. It is not really practical for a timed essay. (Yes, you can brainstorm by yourself.)

Notating the Text

After deconstructing the prompt, the next step is to notate the text, using any of the above techniques that are appropriate and comfortable for you. The notating process demands your active involvement with the text. You need to:

1. Quickly read to get the gist of the text.

Completing items 2 through 5 should not take any longer than 2–3 minutes.

2. Take a moment to clarify your take on the text (your response to subject, tone, style, etc.).
3. Check the title, etc., for any useable peripheral information.
4. Jot down any general thoughts and observations in the top margin area.
5. Go back to the prompt and choose those elements with which you are comfortable and that seem appropriate for the required task.
6. Then, go back to the text for a truly close second reading.

> Carefully completing item 7 will point you in the direction of the development of your essay.

7. Notate those elements, details, examples, etc., that illustrate the devices, techniques, and ideas on which you've chosen to focus.

> With the notated text in front of you, planning the organization of your essay will prove to be a quick and easy task as you complete items 8 through 10.

8. Categorize your notes. This simply means deciding which information you will link to each of the major elements that you're developing.
9. Develop the sequence in which you will present each element or major point.
10. Decide on which examples, details, etc., you will use to develop each element or major idea and in what order you will place specifics.
11. Last, decide on which rhetorical strategy will be your controlling organizational pattern.

> After all of these preliminary steps have been completed, the writer should find it fairly easy to construct a clear and workable thesis statement.

With the prewriting and basic planning completed, you've

- decided what you are going to write about;
- thought about the elements of the prompt you will deal with;
- thought about the purpose of the essay;
- made a decision about the tone you will take.

You're now in a position to construct a thesis statement that makes the reader aware of the writer's assertion and purpose. **In other words, the thesis statement will clearly indicate the subject and controlling idea of the essay.** It should also give the reader some idea as to the pattern of development (rhetorical strategy) and the direction the essay will take in relation to the subject and controlling idea. Here are a few examples of good thesis statements created by AP English students:

- Goodwin and Dickens create two images of the famous London fog **[subject]** that are at radically opposite ends of the "fog spectrum." **[controlling idea]**
- In Alice Walker's novel *The Color Purple,* the heroine, Celie, **[subject]** grows and develops tremendously as an individual as she undergoes major spiritual and psychological transformations. **[controlling idea]**
- Attempting to convince the white man to deal fairly with native Americans, **[subject]** Chief Seattle appeals to the pride and reason of Governor Isaac I. Stevens in a speech that reminds the Governor that, though weak, native Americans are not powerless. **[controlling idea]**

Workout: Self-Control Exercise for Your Own Thesis Statement

1. Locate at least three of your own AP English essays and write down the thesis statement for each.

A. _____

_____

_____

B. _____

_____

_____

C. _____

_____

_____

2. Underline the subject of each thesis statement.
3. Bracket the controlling idea of each thesis statement.

4. Is the subject clear in each statement? _____ yes _____ no

5. Is the controlling idea clear in each statement? _____ yes _____ no

6. If you answered "no" to either number 4 or 5, or both, you need to revise. Don't neglect this or pooh-pooh it. Revision practice can only help your thesis writing skills improve.

Two Sample Texts

Read and think with us as we work our way through this sample text. Pay attention to the notes in the margins and the words, phrases, and sentences in the text that are bracketed. After notating the text, we manipulate these notes into statements about the text, and based on these notes and statements, we write the thesis statement.

AP English Language Sample

A Presidential Candidate
by Mark Twain

as it appeared in *The New York Evening Post* (June 9, 1879)

I have pretty much made up my mind to run for President. What the country wants is a candidate who cannot be injured by investigation of his past history, so that the enemies of the party will be unable to rake up anything against him that nobody ever heard of before. If you know the worst about a candidate, to begin with, every attempt to spring things on him will be checkmated. Now I am going to enter the field with an open record. I am going to own up in advance to all the wickedness I have done, and if any Congressional committee is disposed to prowl around my biography in the hope of discovering any dark and deadly deed that I have secreted, why—let it prowl.

In the first place, I admit that I treed a rheumatic grandfather of mine in the winter of 1850. He was old and inexpert in climbing trees, but with the heartless brutality that is characteristic of me I ran him out of the front door in his nightshirt at the point of a shotgun, and caused him to bowl up a maple tree, where he remained all night, while I emptied shot into his legs. I did this because he snored. I will do it again if I ever have another grandfather. I am as inhuman now as I was in 1850. I candidly acknowledge that I ran away at the battle of Gettysburg. My friends have tried to smooth over this fact by asserting that I did so for the purpose of imitating Washington, who went into the woods at Valley Forge for the purpose of saying his prayers. It was a miserable subterfuge. I struck out in a straight line for the Tropic of Cancer because I was scared. I wanted my country saved, but I preferred to have somebody else save it. I entertain that preference yet. If the bubble reputation can be obtained only at the cannon's mouth, I am willing to go there for it, provided the cannon is empty. If it is loaded my immortal and inflexible purpose is to get over the fence and go home. My invariable practice in war has been to bring out of every fight two-thirds more men than when I went in. This seems to me to be Napoleonic in its grandeur.

My financial views are of the most decided character, but they are not likely, perhaps, to increase my popularity with the advocates of inflation. I do not insist upon the special supremacy of rag money or hard money. The great fundamental principle of my life is to take any kind I can get.

The rumor that I buried a dead aunt under my grapevine was correct. The vine needed fertilizing, my aunt had to be buried, and I dedicated her to this high purpose. Does that unfit me for the Presidency? The Constitution of our country does not say so. No other citizen was ever considered unworthy of this office because he enriched his grapevines with his dead relatives. Why should I be selected as the first victim of an absurd prejudice?

I admit also that I am not a friend of the poor man. I regard the poor man, in his present condition, as so much wasted raw material. Cut up and properly canned, he might be made useful to fatten the natives of the cannibal islands and to improve our export trade with that region. I shall recommend legislation upon the subject in my first message. My campaign cry will be: "Desiccate the poor workingman; stuff him into sausages."

These are about the worst parts of my record. On them I come before the country. If my country don't want me, I will go back again. But I recommend myself as a safe man—a man who starts from the basis of total depravity and proposes to be fiendish to the last.

A Deconstruction of the AP English Language Sample

A Presidential Candidate
by Mark Twain

as it appeared in *The New York Evening Post* (June 9, 1879)

parody
regional I have <u>pretty much made up my mind</u> to run for President. What the country wants is a   non-humorous

candidate who cannot be injured by investigation of his past history, so that the enemies of   honest

the party will be unable to rake up anything against him that nobody ever heard of before. If

will tell his sins

you know the worst about a candidate, to begin with, every attempt to spring things on him will be checkmated. Now I am going to enter the field with an open record. I am going to own up in advance to all the wickedness I have done, and if any Congressional committee is disposed to prowl around my biography in the hope of discovering any dark and deadly deed that I have secreted, why—let it prowl.

regional

regional

experiences

1

In the first place, I admit that I treed a rheumatic grandfather of mine in the winter of 1850. He was old and inexpert in climbing trees, but with the heartless brutality that is characteristic of me I ran him out of the front door in his nightshirt at the point of a shotgun, and caused him to bowl up a maple tree, where he remained all night, while I emptied shot into his legs. I did this because he snored. I will do it again if I ever have another grandfather. I am as inhuman now as I was in 1850. I candidly acknowledge that I ran away at the battle of Gettysburg. My friends have tried to smooth over this fact by asserting that I did so for the purpose of imitating Washington, who went into the woods at Valley Forge for the purpose of saying his prayers. It was a miserable subterfuge. I struck out in a straight line for the Tropic of Cancer because I was scared. I wanted my country saved, but I preferred to have somebody else save it. I entertain that preference yet. If the bubble reputation can be obtained only at the cannon's mouth, I am willing to go there for it, provided the cannon is empty. If it is loaded my immortal and inflexible purpose is to get over the fence and go home. My invariable practice in war has been to bring out of every fight two-thirds more men than when I went in. This seems to me to be Napoleonic in its grandeur.

family tale

exaggerates

improbable

historical

references

war tale

war experience

exaggeration

and

irony

exaggeration

economic view

My financial views are of the most decided character, but they are not likely, perhaps, to increase my popularity with the advocates of inflation. I do not insist upon the special supremacy of rag money or hard money. The great fundamental principle of my life is to take any kind I can get.

opinion

2nd family tale

irony and sarcasm

The rumor that I buried a dead aunt under my grapevine was correct. The vine needed fertilizing, my aunt had to be buried, and I dedicated her to this high purpose. Does that unfit me for the Presidency? The Constitution of our country does not say so. No other citizen was ever considered unworthy of this office because he enriched his grapevines with his dead relatives. Why should I be selected as the first victim of an absurd prejudice?

rhetorical

questions opinion

opinion re: the common man

I admit also that I am not a friend of the poor man. I regard the poor man, in his present condition, as so much wasted raw material. Cut up and properly canned, he might be made useful to fatten the natives of the cannibal islands and to improve our export trade with that region. I shall recommend legislation upon the subject in my first message. My campaign cry will be: "Desiccate the poor workingman; stuff him into sausages."

opposite views

allusion to "A Modest Proposal"

informal These are about the worst parts of my record. On them I come before the country. If my country don't want me, I will go back again. But I recommend myself as a safe man—a man who starts from the basis of total depravity and proposes to be fiendish to the last.

total opposite of how politicians end their speeches

Using the notes, the writer can easily complete each of the following planning points.

1. The purpose of "A Presidential Candidate" is to parody campaign speeches.
2. The tone/attitude of the selection is sarcastic, ironic, humorous.
3. The rhetorical devices used to develop the purpose and attitude include:

DEVICE	LOCATION
1. exaggeration	1. ¶2-grandfather, ¶4-aunt, ¶5-the poor
2. irony	2. ¶2-war exp., ¶3-finance, ¶4-burial
3. choice of details	3. (see irony) ¶2-Washington, ¶4-Constitution, ¶5-allusion
4. informal diction	4. ¶1-"pretty much own up . . ." ¶1-"prowl around," ¶2-"bowl up," ¶6-". . . don't want me"
5. rhetorical questions	5. ¶2 (2 examples)

3. "A Presidential Candidate" resembles a typical speech made by a political candidate today in several ways: (1) references to personal and moral standing, (2) family background, (3) position on the economy, (4) position on the common man, and (5) war experiences and patriotism.

4. "A Presidential Candidate" does NOT resemble a typical speech made by a political candidate today in several ways. First, rather than emphasizing the "good," he's done, Twain focuses on the "wrongs" he's committed. Second, he takes the absurdly opposite positions on the usual political issues. Third, rather than lofty language, his diction is informal and folksy.

Using the above information, the writer is in a position to write a clear **thesis statement.**

> In "A Presidential Candidate," Mark Twain makes his own "modest proposal"
> [subject] with a parody of the typical political campaign speech. [controlling idea]

AP English Literature Sample

As we did with the previous sample, read and think with us as we work our way through this sample poem. Pay attention to the notes in the margins and the words, phrases and lines that are bracketed. After notating the text, we manipulate these notes into statements about the poem, and based on these notes and statements, we write the thesis statement.

Dover Beach by Matthew Arnold (1867)

The sea is calm tonight,
The tide is full, the moon lies fair
Upon the straits; on the French coast the light
Gleams and is gone; the cliffs of England stand,
Glimmering and vast, out in the tranquil bay.
Come to the window, sweet is the night air!
Only, from the long line of spray

5

Where the sea meets the moon-blanched land,

Listen! you hear the grating roar

Of pebbles which the waves draw back, and fling,   10

At their return, up the high strand,

Begin, and cease, and then again begin,

With tremulous cadence slow, and bring

The eternal note of sadness in.

Sophocles long ago   15

Heard it on the Aegean, and it brought

Into his mind the turbid ebb and flow

Of human misery; we

Find also in the sound a thought,

Hearing it by this distant northern sea.   20

The Sea of Faith

Was once, too, at the full, and round earth's shore

Lay like the folds of a bright girdle furled.

But now I only hear

Its melancholy, long, withdrawing roar,   25

Retreating, to the breath

Of the night wind, down the vast edges drear

And naked shingles of the world.

Ah, love, let us be true

To one another! for the world, which seems   30

To lie before us like a land of dreams,

So various, so beautiful, so new,

Hath really neither joy, nor love, nor light,

Nor certitude, nor peace, nor help for pain;

And we are here as on a darkling plain   35

Swept with confused alarms of struggle and flight,

Where ignorant armies clash by night.

A Deconstruction of the AP English Literature Sample

Dover Beach by Matthew Arnold (1867)

Positive

Sea = calm/full/ The sea is calm to-night,   **Positive**

tranquil   **night = moon/fair/light/**

The tide is full, the moon lies fair   **gleams/glimmering**

Upon the straits; on the French coast the light

Gleams and is gone; the cliffs of England stand,

Glimmering and vast, out in the tranquil bay.   5

Look!--- Come to the window, sweet is the night air!   **sweet-night**

senses Only, from the long line of spray

Where the sea meets the moon-blanched land,   **contrast–sea & land**

Listen--- | Listen! you hear the grating roar | onomatopoeia

Of pebbles which the waves draw back, and fling, | 10

At their return, up the high strand,

Begin, and cease, and then again begin, | caesuras & enjambment

Meter is slow With tremulous cadence slow, and bring | for contrast

The eternal note of sadness in. | go/stop/go pattern

why?--- Sophocles long ago | 15

Heard it on the Aegean, and it brought-------------- allusion

Into his mind the turbid ebb and flow | contrast

what sadness? Of human misery; we

Find also in the sound a thought,

Hearing it by this distant northern sea. | 20

Negative The Sea of Faith | **Negative**

Sea = turbid/distant/ Was once, too, at the full, and round earth's shore | **night = drear/naked**

misery/north Lay like the folds of a bright girdle furled.

But now I only hear

Its melancholy, long, withdrawing roar, | assonance-sound/ slow | 25

Retreating, to the breath

Of the night wind, down the vast edges drear

And naked shingles* of the world.

Ah, love, let us be true ------------------------------- ** theme—his plea**

To one another! for the world, which seems | not real—dreams | 30

To lie before us like a land of dreams,

So various, so beautiful, so new,

Hath really neither joy, nor love, nor light, | repetition and contrast

Nor certitude, nor peace, nor help for pain; | positive to negative

Simile in last 3 lines And we are here as on a darkling plain | 35

Swept with confused alarms of struggle and flight,

Where ignorant armies clash by night.

contrast—sea to
land starts and ends
with night/no light

*shingles = beaches

Using the notes written in the margins of the poem, the writer easily constructs the following mapping/chart.

CONTRASTS

Sea / **Land** (Diction and Imagery)

stanza 1 {
calm	confused
light	darkling
tranquil	struggle & clash
} *stanza 4*

stanza 2 { Sophocles/Aegean long ago / Lovers / Northern sea now

Sea	of	**Faith**
↓		↓
once		now
↓		↓
full, bright		melancholy, drear
} *stanza 3*

Land, of dreams /	**Land of reality**
|	|
so various	neither joy
so beautiful	nor love
so new	nor light
	nor certitude
	nor peace
	nor help for pain
} *stanza 4, repetition*

DEVICES / TECHNIQUES

Caesura—lines 9–12—all of stanzas 1 and 4
  Begin/cease/begin (contrast)
  go/stop/go = the waves
Enjambment—lines 15–20—longer cadence = thoughts
Metaphor—lines 20–27—Sea of Faith = disillusionment
Simile—lines 29–36—like a land of dreams + as on a darkling plain (contrast)

THEMES

Life is a battle.   ------}   Only love is
Life is ebb and flow.   constantly in contrast
Life is universal.   to war/misery/darkness

OBSERVATIONS

Moves from positive to negative
Moves from specific to universal to specific
Moves from light to dark
Moves from look to listen
ebb & flow of sea = ebb/flow of their love

climax = lines 27–28: his appeal that love is the only contrast to misery and pain.
    love and loving are the only certainties in life.

Using the above information, the writer is in a position to write a clear **thesis statement.**

Matthew Arnold's poem "Dover Beach" is a study in contrasts **[subject]** *developed to convince his beloved of the value of love and loyalty.* **[controlling idea]**

A Note About Note-Taking Styles

You have no doubt noticed that the notation, prewriting, and planning styles of the two samples above are quite different. (At least, we hope you've noticed.) This was done purposely to illustrate the very important point that **there is no single, correct way to read, notate, prewrite, and plan any essay.** The important factor here is that you do the close reading, etc., and that you do it using strategies and techniques that are comfortable for you. As the old Nike ad said, "Just do it!"

With the prewriting and planning completed, you're ready to write your essay.

STEP 4

Review the Knowledge You Need to Get a High Score

CHAPTER > 8

Introducing the Essay

IN THIS CHAPTER

Summary: Examine effective techniques for introducing the subject of your essay

Key Ideas
✪ Practice with the topic and purpose you will present
✪ Develop your assertion and how you will appeal to your specific audience
✪ Read professional introductions and commentary
✪ Practice writing effective introductions

"Composing is not a linear process, though what it creates has linear form."
—Anne Berthoff, *The Making of Meaning*

Composing has its peaks and valleys, ups and downs, circuitous and bumpy highways and byways, and getting from point A to point Z can be like walking or driving backward. However, the important thing is to arrive at your destination with both you and your reader safely intact.

One of the important steps to help smooth out the literary ride is to create a clear, informative, and interesting opening paragraph. By now, you have had experiences with many English instructors who have correctly told you that an introduction has a specific job to do. And, by now, you must feel that you're fairly expert at constructing these opening salvos for your essays.

However, humor your trainers, and take a few moments to review what you've been taught in the past. **Specifically the introductory paragraph or opening should indicate:**

- What is to follow;
- The topic you will address;
- Your position on the subject;
- Why the reader should be at all interested in the subject;
- Why your reader should pay any attention to your take on this subject.

In other words, you, the writer, have to make your intentions clear, grab your reader's interest and imply the significance of your subject.

You've also practiced many times over the "formula" for the construction of the opening paragraph. **An introductory paragraph must contain an introduction to the subject plus any needed background information, such as dates, statistics, scenario, etc., plus an indication of the organizational pattern of the essay plus a thesis statement.**

Okay. So, supposedly, you know what your writing job is and how it should be accomplished. If that is true, why bother strengthening your skills for writing the introduction? Why? Because you're maturing as a writer, and you want to be treated and taken seriously as an adult writer with something interesting to say about important topics. There's more to the writing life than three-word sentences and five-sentence paragraphs. There's a whole world of adventurous openings just waiting for you to write them and curious readers whose interests can be piqued.

You're also familiar with the old cliché "You can't judge a book by its cover." But, let's be honest here. No matter how hard we may try not to, we DO draw immediate conclusions about people, events, presentations, etc., based on the initial impression or impact on us. And, when it comes to writing, a reader is quick to throw down or ignore a text that does not capture his or her attention within the first few lines. Therefore, YOU, THE WRITER, have to grab the attention of your intended reader in that introductory paragraph or section.

We say introductory paragraph or section because the length of your introduction depends on the length of the entire text. A short essay needs one opening paragraph, perhaps two at times. However, a longer work such as a research paper demands several paragraphs, and a book may require an entire chapter or two. No matter the text and the length of the introduction, it is important to ease your reader into the subject. Get them comfortable in the passenger seat and strap them in for the ride.

There are several techniques for introducing the subject of your essay. These include:

- **Analogy** _____ Present a comparison between your subject and something with which your reader is most probably familiar.

- **Anecdote** _____ Choose a brief incident that relates to your subject and tells the story.

- **Dialogue** _____ Include a brief piece of conversation that is related to your subject and that will lead to your assertion.

- **Explicit and direct statement of the assertion** _____ Go right to the subject and assertion of your essay and state it clearly. This type of opening is especially useful for those writing assignments that are reports, essays in science or history, or for essay assignments that present difficulties to both you and your reader.

- **Interesting fact or detail** _____ Choose an interesting historical reference, a statistic, or a specific detail and indicate how it is related to your subject.

- **Question** _____ Ask a broad question and indicate how it could be related to your subject/assertion. The question can be a regular question for which you will provide an answer, or it could be rhetorical.

- **Quotation** _____ Find a quotation that is related to your subject and indicate how it is related to your thesis. Quotations can come from within the text being discussed or from another source.

- **Startling remark** _____ This should be a real attention grabber. However, make certain that it is actually related to your subject and your assertion about it.

> Remember that no matter which opening gambit you choose to employ, that introduction should be one that is specifically tuned to your subject, assertion, purpose, and audience.

How The Professionals Do It

Let's take a close look at a series of introductions written by professionals. Writers of fiction and nonfiction frequently use the same techniques to involve their readers. Just as we often jump to conclusions about individuals or situations based on first impressions, so, too, do readers often jump to conclusions about continuing to read a work. It is imperative for an author to capture and coerce his or her reader to be actively involved from the beginning. Take a look at these examples, both fiction and nonfiction, and concentrate on the writer's craft as you read.

J. D. Salinger from *The Catcher in the Rye*

> *If you really want to hear about it, the first thing you'll probably want to know is where I was born, and what my lousy childhood was like, and how my parents were occupied and all before they had me, and all that David Copperfield kind of crap, but I don't feel like going into it, if you really want to know the truth.*

Comments: (question)

This first person opening draws the reader into the passage by posing an implied question on the part of the reader—if you really want to hear about it—and then by answering it—I don't feel like going into it—thereby raising the reader's curiosity. Stylistically, the speaker mixes literary allusion and colloquialisms, indicating a complex character. The concept of truth hints at the thematic elements of the novel.

Mark Twain from *The Adventures of Huckleberry Finn*

> *You don't know about me, without you have read a book by the name of "The Adventures of Tom Sawyer," but that ain't no matter. That book was made by Mr. Mark Twain, and he told the truth, mainly. There was things which he stretched, but mainly he told the truth. That is nothing. I never seen anybody but lied, one time or another, without it was Aunt Polly, or the widow, or maybe Mary. Aunt Polly, Tom's Aunt Polly she is—and Mary, and the Widow Douglas, is all told about in that book—which is mostly a true book; with some stretchers, as I said before.*

Comments: (dialogue)

Here is one of the most famous openings in all of American literature. Twain's first person narrative is made immediately compelling as Huck introduces himself to the reader. The reference to *The Adventures of Tom Sawyer* and to Twain, himself; the informality and regional English; plus Huck's obvious desire to tell his story, all provide a sense of time and place and draw the audience into the story.

Rita Mae Brown from *Rita Will: Memoir of a Literary Rabble-Rouser*

My mother was mucking stalls at Hanover Shoe Farm outside of Hanover, Pennsylvania, within a shout of the Mason–Dixon line, when her water broke. Had the hospital not been nearby, I would have been born in a manger. Perhaps I came into the world knowing Jesus had already done that, and since he suffered for all of us I saw no reason to be redundant.

Comments: (anecdote)
Ms. Brown's first person anecdote introduces herself to the reader as a straight-talking, ironic and humorous individual. It also lets the reader know that this is going to be a type of memoir.

F. Scott Fitzgerald from *The Great Gatsby*

In my younger and more vulnerable years my father gave me some advice that I've been turning over in my mind ever since.

"Whenever you feel like criticizing any one," he told me, "just remember that all the people in this world haven't had the advantages that you've had."

He didn't say any more, but we've always been unusually communicative in a reserved way, and I understood that he meant a great deal more than that. In consequence, I'm inclined to reserve all judgments, a habit that has opened up many curious natures to me and also made me the victim of not a few veteran bores.

Comments: (quotation and anecdote)
This opening employs a quotation and an anecdote to introduce the themes of the novel and the narrator. The reader infers that judgment, consequences, communication, vulnerability and victimization will all be important in this work.

Jane Austen from *Pride and Prejudice*

It is a truth universally acknowledged, that a single man in possession of a good fortune must be in want of a wife. However little known the feelings or views of such a man may be on his first entering a neighborhood, this truth is so well fixed in the minds of the surrounding families, that he is considered as the rightful property of someone or other of their daughters.

Comments: (explicit statement)
The opening sentence is also the assertion upon which the novel is developed. There is no doubt in the reader's mind about the subject matter or focus of the novel. The pleasant surprise is the understated humor in the first paragraph which alludes to a witty and wry tone toward the subject.

Thomas Jefferson from *The Declaration of Independence*

When in the course of human events, it becomes necessary for one people to dissolve the political bands which have connected them with another, and to assume among the powers of the earth, the separate and equal station to which the Laws of Nature and of Nature's God entitle them, a decent respect to the opinions of mankind requires that they should declare the causes which impel them to the separation.

Comments: (direct plus explicit)

In his opening, Jefferson is forceful and direct. Without hyperbolic language, or interesting tales and references, he makes it clear to the world the exact purpose and assertion of his declaration.

Richard Wright from *Native Son*

> *Brrrrrrriiiiiiiiiiiiiiiinnng!*
>> *An alarm clock clanged in the dark and silent room. A bed spring creaked.*
>> *A woman's voice sang out impatiently: "Bigger, shut that thing off!"*

Comments: (dialogue)

This tidbit of dialogue, as emphatic as the alarm clock itself, emphasizes the demands made on the main character who has yet to be met. The brevity of the introduction and the simplicity of syntax and diction establish the elemental quality of the work.

Albert Camus from *The Stranger*

> *Mother died today. Or, maybe, yesterday; I can't be sure. The telegram from the Home says: YOUR MOTHER PASSED AWAY. FUNERAL TOMORROW. DEEP SYMPATHY. Which leaves the matter doubtful; it could have been yesterday.*

Comments: (startling remark)

Certainly this novel opens with a startling observation. Perhaps it is the objectivity of the speaker that is so shocking and compelling that we must read on. On another level, the opening is analogous to the entire existential movement: death, uncertainty, isolation, the inadequacy of communication and the absurdity of time and life, are the basic tenets of the philosophy Camus will explore in the novel.

Calvin Trillin from "Comforting Thoughts" in *Enough's Enough (And Other Rules of Life)*

> *First I read a study in Meriden, Connecticut, which indicated that talking to yourself is a perfectly legitimate way of getting comfort during a difficult time. Then I saw an item about research at Yale demonstrating that stress seems to be reduced in some people by exposing them to aromas of certain desserts. Then I started talking to myself about desserts with aromas I find soothing. Then I felt a lot better. Isn't science grand?*

Comments: (interesting facts plus rhetorical question)

Mr. Trillin's citing of the two research studies and his use of the rhetorical question to end the opening paragraph easily and humorously indicate the subject, the assertion and the tone the essay will take.

Louisa May Alcott from *Little Women*

> *"Christmas won't be Christmas without any presents," grumbled Jo, lying on the rug.*
>> *"It's so dreadful to be poor!" sighed Meg, looking down at her old dress.*
>> *"I don't think it's fair for some girls to have plenty of pretty things and other girls nothing at all," added little Amy, with an injured sniff.*
>> *"We've got father and mother and each other," said Beth contentedly, from her corner.*

Comments: (dialogue)

Totally dependent on dialogue, this opening introduces four diverse characters with incredible economy. Each personality is defined, the conflicts are enumerated, the ideal is presented, and the reader is given the opportunity to identify with the speaker of his choice.

David Sedaris's Opening of "Diary of a Smoker" in *Barrel Fever*

> *I rode my bike to the boat pond in Central Park, where I bought myself a cup of coffee and sat down on a bench to read. I lit a cigarette and was enjoying myself when the woman seated twelve feet away, on the other side of the bench, began waving her hands before her face. I thought she was fighting off a bee.*
>
> *She fussed at the air and called out, "Excuse me, do you mind if we make this a no-smoking bench?"*

Comments: (dialogue plus anecdote)

David Sedaris uses this first person anecdote that includes dialogue to introduce the reader to both his subject and his assertion. It is obvious to any reader that Mr. Sedaris is not at all happy with those who would impose their no-smoking mania on others.

Camille Paglia from "Rock as Art" in *Sex, Art and American Culture*

> *Rock is eating its young. Rock musicians are America's most wasted natural resource.*

Comments: (analogy plus startling statement)

Containing two startling analogies, this quite brief pair of sentences is the opening salvo to an essay in which Ms. Paglia will obviously be arguing in favor of the importance of "rock."

Opening Paragraphs

As a first example, the writer for our Mark Twain prompt has written the following three opening paragraphs.

A

Honesty and *politics*. For the cynic in each of us, these are two mutually exclusive terms. Each time we hear a politician say, "I want to be perfectly clear," we know to take what is said with a grain of salt. Mark Twain plays with our political cynicism in "A Presidential Candidate," an essay that parodies the stereotypical campaign speech.

B

We've all heard the following before, haven't we? "Trust me. I only want to be your public servant. I will always work for the common good of all." It's so familiar and so shallow that the political cynic in each of us responds, "*Sure* we should. *Sure* he does. *Sure* he will." Aware of this cynicism, Mark Twain plays with our political suspicions in "A Presidential Candidate," a parody of the typical campaign speech.

C

Barely 51 percent of those eligible to vote did so in the last presidential election. Do you wonder why? Perhaps it's the result of voters distrusting politicians. Mark Twain plays with this cynicism of the electorate in "A Presidential Candidate," an essay that parodies the stereotypical political campaign speech.

Comments

Opening **A** uses a brief quotation to introduce the context of the essay; whereas, opening **B** employs a rhetorical question and two bits of dialogue to grab the reader's attention and to indicate the subject. Last, opening **C** presents an interesting, if not startling, statistic and a rhetorical question to engage and lead the reader to the assertion. After thoughtfully considering each of these introductions and the purpose of the essay, our writer has chosen to use opening **B.** This is a choice that could certainly be changed in a writing situation that allows for revision. However, in a timed essay exam, opening **B** would be our first AND final choice because it lends itself most directly to both the assertion and the tone the writer wishes to take.

For our second example, the writer for the "Dover Beach" prompt has composed the following three opening paragraphs.

A

"Ah, love, let us be true to one another!" says Matthew Arnold. What a line! One can almost hear him asking his beloved what her sign is. And yet, this impassioned and shameless plea for requited love works, and it works because of the diction, poetic devices, and imagery Arnold presents in "Dover Beach." The poor girl doesn't have a chance.

B

From "calm to clash, from light to darkling, from sea to land," Matthew Arnold's poem "Dover Beach" is a study in contrast. This contrast is necessary to convince his love to be true, and it is developed throughout the poem by an increasingly negative progression of examples. This organizational pattern is enhanced by the form and structure of the lines. Arnold also appeals to the senses to bring his love to see the urgency of his desire and passion. The metaphors and allusions all reiterate his position, that love and lovemaking are the only things of certainty in an ignorant and hostile world.

C

It seems there is nothing new under the sun after all. Whenever young men are endangered by war, they are driven to counter the threat of death with the experience of life. In *A Streetcar Named Desire,* Blanche DuBois says "the opposite of death is desire" and this seems especially appropriate to remember when reading Matthew Arnold's poem, "Dover Beach." Through poetic devices, symbols, and repetition, the poet argues for love and fidelity.

Comments

All three opening paragraphs include author, title, and genre. Each addresses the major points of the prompt and indicates the writer's understanding of task and text. Opening **A** refers to a quotation from the poem to help establish the voice of the writer. The tone of the essay is clear and engaging. Opening **B** immediately makes reference to the entire poem with specific details and delineates the direction the essay will take. It is clear and academic and indicates a level of confidence on the part of the writer. Opening **C** links one literary work with another and incorporates an outside quotation to illustrate an analogous insight about the poem.

In a timed situation, the writer would be most comfortable developing example **B** because it already has established the format of the essay. Sequence and progression help to control literary analysis and keep the writer on track. Example **A** might be more fun to write, but it could be difficult to maintain tone, and the desire to be clever could get in the way of the task. Likewise, opening **C** could prove limiting because of its focus on the last stanza as the controlling idea. Each of these openings would be suitable for an untimed essay, but for this, opening **B** is the choice.

Student Samples

Professional writers make their living doing this kind of stuff, but what about the ordinary student who is stuck writing an essay in answer to a specific assignment or prompt? To find out, read the following student samples.

Student A

The culmination of moral reconciliation and spiritual awakening is most evident at the end of Toni Morrison's Song of Solomon. *This gradual enlightenment, rather than a sudden epiphany, is portrayed through Milkman, the heroic character of the novel.*

Comments

This brief, but on-target, introduction indicates a student writer who is in control of his or her subject. Not only does the writer state the subject and purpose of the essay, but he or she also employs mature diction and presents insights using phrases such as *moral reconciliation and spiritual awakening,* and *rather than a sudden epiphany* to point out an inherent contrast.

Student B

In her op-ed piece, "Pretty Poison," Maureen Dowd examines and modifies Anna Quindlen's earlier insight into the categorized life span of a woman, that is, "pre-Babe, Babe, and post-Babe." Reflecting on the new "Botox-injection craze," Dowd facetiously updates Quindlen's classifications to, "pre-Babe, Babe, Botox-Babe, and Cher." Ms. Dowd employs a variety of rhetorical devices to expose the absurdity of the female ideal of presenting herself as a younger, more attractive woman than she believes she is.

Comments

This introduction clearly presents both the subject and purpose together with the writer's definite attitude toward Ms. Dowd's and Ms. Quindlen's topics that this student refers to with quotations from the op-ed column. Using words such as *craze, facetiously,* and *absurdity,* the reader also becomes aware of an upcoming "prickly" analysis of the columnist's presentation.

Student C

The reader of Norman Mailer's passage walks away with great empathy for Benny "Kid" Paret and a better understanding of what it was like in that arena the night of his massacre. Mailer's diction, syntax, and use of specific animal imagery recreates this event with a dichotomous tone and a sense of the bestiality of the "sweet science."

Comments

Here is a student who has a definite point of view and is not afraid to make that point of view known to the reader who is brought immediately into the essay. The writer's tone is obvious from the very beginning with the use of words such as *massacre,* and *bestiality,* and, the thesis incorporates the prompt without a bland restatement of its purpose and object.

Student D

In sixth grade, when most boys fantasize about becoming famous baseball players, I dreamed, among other things, about being a contestant on Jeopardy. Athletics interested me, but I suspected that fame and fortune would be more assured if I pursued the game show route. Now, six years later, I was actually auditioning for Teen Jeopardy. At last, I would have the opportunity to mentally spar with the other contestants and relate my own droll anecdote to Alex Trebek. Dreams can come true.

Comments

This is an intriguing opening to a personal essay. The student's use of anecdote immediately sets the informal and personal tone of the essay as it piques the reader's curiosity. Will the writer's dream come true? What happened on *Teen Jeopardy*?

Total Workout

Enough of just looking at others. It's time to stretch and maximize your own opening skills.

Go to your writing folder or portfolio and choose THREE opening paragraphs.

- Either rewrite or copy and paste each of the openings on a separate sheet of paper and answer the following questions:

  1. The subject of the essay is _____
  _____.

  2. My purpose is _____.

  3. My audience is _____.

  4. My assertion is _____.

  5. I used the following opening technique(s) in my opening _____
  _____.

  6. I believe the opening is good just the way it is. _____ yes _____ no

  7. If you answered "no" to question 6, what technique do you think would be a better choice?_____.

- Choose ONE of the introductions and complete the following:

  1. Using three different techniques, rewrite the opening THREE different ways below.

  Technique _____ Rewrite: _____
  _____
  _____

_____

_____

_____

_____

Technique _____ Rewrite: _____

_____

_____

_____

_____

_____

Technique _____ Rewrite: _____

_____

_____

_____

_____

_____

_____

2. Which technique do you think works best? _____

3. Why do you believe this method is best? _____

4. Ask one of your peers to read each opening and see whether or not he or she agrees with your choice.

5. Do you think revising your introduction would make your essay even better? _____ yes _____ no. Why? _____

_____

Can you feel the burn? Well, before you cool down, here's another item to consider when deciding on your opening. If you are given a writing assignment that involves several classes and several steps, from planning to first draft to peer review to revision, you can take a great deal of time to consider and reconsider your introduction. This is the time to experiment and to be creative. However, in a timed situation, you will have to think quickly and decisively. The more practice you allow yourself in the untimed essays, the better you will be in the stressful and demanding timed writing environments.

> You can read the complete essays by our two sample writers at the end of Chapter 10.

CHAPTER ▶ 9

Constructing the Body of the Essay and Supporting Syntax

IN THIS CHAPTER

Summary: Understand different organizational patterns and the role of syntax

KEY IDEA

Key Ideas
- ✪ Practice with each of the major patterns
- ✪ Examine professional examples and commentary
- ✪ Review student samples and commentary
- ✪ Practice with your own writing
- ✪ Practice with transition, annotation, and voice

"What is written without effort is read without pleasure."
—Samuel Johnson

Yes! We are going to acknowledge that you have been putting in a great deal of effort so far. But, the operative phrase here is "so far." You've only just begun. With the close reading, prewriting, planning, and introduction completed, you're set to write the body of your essay.

Don't doubt yourself. You ARE ready to write the body of your essay. You know your audience, your purpose, your assertion, and your rhetorical strategy. You know the major points that support your assertion, you know the sequence of your specific examples that illustrate each of your major points, and you've engaged your reader. Now what?

Here's what—decide on your organizing principle. That's the basic pattern that you'll use to develop your presentation. You're already familiar with these patterns; you've been using them for years. You just need to put them in specific context. **Each rhetorical strategy lends itself to a specific organizational structure.** These are:

- **Chronological order** deals with items in the time order in which they occur. The two strategies that use this pattern are **narration** and **process**.
- **Spatial order** details items as they appear in a particular environment: from right to left, top to bottom, front to back, etc. This pattern is most often used in **description**.
- **Subject by subject** discusses each subject in a separate paragraph or section.
- **Point by point** examines each point in a separate paragraph or section.

These patterns are used with **contrast/comparison**.

- **Categorizing** is the process of placing items in groups and examining each one of the categories and the items in it. Obviously, the rhetorical strategy that demands this pattern is **classification**.
- **A single cause leading to a single effect or multiple effects**
- **Multiple causes leading to a single effect or multiple effects**
- **A single effect and the single or multiple cause(s)**
- **Multiple effects and the single or multiple cause(s)**

These patterns are best used for the *cause/effect* strategy

- **Most important to least important or vice versa** can be used to organize almost any of the rhetorical strategies, especially analysis, explanation and *cause/effect*.
- **Deduction** is a pattern that works from the general (thesis) to specific/supporting details, while **induction** works from the specific examples/details to the general (thesis). **Argumentation** is the strategy that most often consciously employs these two patterns.

> The organizational pattern is usually given to the writer in the very wording of the timed AP English essay prompt. However, when you are given a writing assignment that does not call for a specific type of organizational pattern, you will have to decide on the best one, based on your thinking, prewriting and planning.

Remember that each major point must play an important part in developing and supporting your assertion. In most instances, you discuss, analyze each major point, and support or illustrate it with specific examples, statistics, details, textual references, etc.

For each point:

- **Introduce it.**
- **Describe it.**
- **Discuss how it is connected to the assertion/claim/thesis.**

You always want to be aware of your thesis, your purpose, and your audience. Each paragraph in the body of your essay has to move your reader closer and closer to your goal, your final destination (your assertion), and you've got to do this making certain to show the interconnectedness among each of your major points with what we call "connective tissue," and what others term transitional elements.

Samples of the Body of the Essay

AP English Language

"A Presidential Candidate"

Informal diction contributes to the overall humor of this parody. Most of us expect a modicum of seriousness and dignity from our political candidates. And, we expect this to be evident in their speeches and writing. To the contrary, Twain uses "folksy" and regional words and phrases throughout the essay. In paragraph one, avoiding lofty language, the author writes "pretty much made up my mind" to tell his audience that he has made a decision, and he invites congressional scrutiny with "let it prowl." Paragraph two has Twain's grandfather "bowling up" a tree when he is chased from his house by the narrator. Using his own method to appeal to the common man, the candidate says, "If my country don't want me. . . ."

Exaggeration also plays a major role in the creation of this humorous takeoff on campaign speeches. The anecdote about the author and his grandfather is in every way over the top. Treeing and shooting his grandfather with buckshot is both ludicrous and highly improbable. The absurdity continues in paragraph four with the tale of his burying his dead aunt "under my grapevine." In paragraph five, Twain takes a wide and caustic swing at political candidates who promise to stand up for the common man. He says, ". . . I regard the poor man, in his present condition, as so much wasted raw material." The author's outrageous suggestion to kill and cannibalize "the poor workingman . . ." and ". . . stuff him into sausages," would have made Jonathan Swift very proud.

Almost all of Twain's selection of details contributes to the irony of this piece. We expect heroic details of the candidate's war experiences, but this candidate describes and admits his cowardice in the face of battle, even while making a tongue-in-cheek reference to Washington. Instead of claiming to be a financial virgin as most candidates do, Twain readily characterizes himself as money hungry and willing to get it any way he can. Adding to the irony that is the basis for the announcement, Twain makes references to the U.S. Constitution and asks rhetorical questions about both his fitness for the presidency and his being a "victim of absurd prejudices."

Analysis of the Body of the Essay

topic sentence Informal diction contributes to the overall humor of this parody. Most of us expect a **transition**

modicum of seriousness and dignity from our political candidates. And, we expect this to be

evident in their speeches and writing. To the contrary, Twain uses "folksy" and regional words

and phrases throughout the essay. In paragraph one, avoiding lofty language, the author

ex. 1 writes "pretty much made up my mind" to tell his audience that he has made a decision, and

ex. 2 he invites congressional scrutiny with "let it prowl." Paragraph two has Twain's grandfather

ex. 3 "bowling up" a tree when he is chased from his house by the narrator. And, in his final

paragraph, the author uses his own method to appeal to the common man when says, "If my

ex. 4 country don't want me . . ."

topic sentence   Exaggeration also plays a major role in the creation of this humorous takeoff on campaign speeches. The anecdote about the author and his grandfather is in everyway

ex. 1 over-the-top. Treeing and shooting his grandfather with buckshot is both ludicrous and

ex. 2 highly improbable. The absurdity continues in paragraph four with the tale of his burying his dead aunt "under my grapevine." In paragraph five, Twain takes a wide and caustic swing

ex. 3 at political candidates who promise to stand up for the common man. He says, ". . . I regard

ex. 4 the poor man, in his present condition, as so much wasted raw material." The author's

good allusion outrageous suggestion to kill and cannibalize "the poor workingman . . ." and ". . . stuff him into sausages," would have made **Jonathan Swift very proud.**

topic sentence   Almost all of Twain's selection of details contributes to the irony of this piece. [We expect heroic tales of the candidate's war experiences, but this candidate describes and

ex. 1 & 2 admits his cowardice in the face of battle, even while making a tongue-in-cheek reference to Washington. Instead of claiming to be a financial virgin, as most candidates do, Twain

ex. 3 readily characterizes himself as money hungry and willing to get it any way he can.] Adding

ex. 4 to the irony that is the basis for the announcement, Twain makes references to the U.S. Constitution and asks rhetorical questions about both his fitness for the presidency and his

ex. 5 & 6 being a "victim of absurd prejudices."

Comments

Because this is an AP English prompt that demands a specific type of response, the body paragraphs almost organize themselves. Pay close attention to the topic sentences, each of which markedly refer the reader to the thesis of the essay. Notice that each of the major points is developed using specific references to the text. For example, the first body paragraph contains four examples of informal diction, each of which is connected to the idea of humor and parody. The second body paragraph discusses the exaggeration Twain employs with three specific references to the text. The last major point concerns irony, and the writer examines this device by citing six textual references.

It is important to note that the textual references are NOT merely listed. They are incorporated into the framework of the paragraph, via both citations and comments, to support and illustrate each topic sentence (underlined). As an example, look carefully at the second and third sentences of paragraph three (bracketed). Including the reader in the comments, the writer vests the audience in the subject and tone of "A Presidential Candidate" and in the AP English essay, itself.

Last, the continuity is maintained throughout with clear transitions and echo words—what we term connecting tissue (blocked). Repeating key words *humor* and *parody* ties the first body paragraph to the opening paragraph. *Also* and *this,* together with the phrase *humorous takeoff,* refer to the previous paragraphs and are, therefore, the key transitions in the second paragraph. Connecting the third paragraph to the prompt and the other preceding paragraphs are the transitional words *Twain's* and *this piece.* Rather than repeating Mark Twain over and over, the writer uses echo words, such as *author, narrator, this candidate.* And, Twain's essay is referred to as *announcement, remarks, absurdity, caustic swing, parody, takeoff.*

AP English Literature

"Dover Beach"

Drawing his images from nature, Arnold creates a romantic scene that will later be contrasted in the final stanza. As he implores his love to look from the window at the world beneath them, the poet introduces the sea and the land, and the diction positions them as the dominant contradictory symbols of the poem. Although it is night, "moon, fair, light, gleams, and glimmering" all illuminate the "calm, full, and tranquil bay." And yet, in his description of the "sweet night," Arnold includes the word, "only" to imply something other than the idyllic vision. This change in mood is meant to make his beloved uneasy, so she will be receptive to him later when he proposes an antidote to the ensuing negative examples.

To further his position, Arnold juxtaposes the sea and the "moon-blanched land," light and dark, and seeing and hearing. Now he orders his love to "Listen!" as well as look. This imperative is also for the reader, and we can hear, through onomatopoeia, the "grating roar" of the pebbles breaking the quiet tone. The following lines, 10–14, depend on sound devices and punctuation to develop contrast. A succession of caesuras breaks the iambic meter and makes the speaker and reader start and stop and start again, much like the rhythm of the waves themselves which "begin, and cease, and then again, begin." Perhaps, Arnold is using this pattern as a parallel to the lovers' relationship. It, too, may have its high and low tides.

Allusions to Sophocles and the Aegean allow Arnold to move from the immediate and specific images of the first stanza to a more general argument. Like the eternal sea, human misery is a common experience, and this example from the past will make his argument for loyalty and love more poignant and universal. His diction now is negative; the sea is "turbid, distant and northern." It is possible his love has also been remote and cold. Again, one can infer that the "ebb and flow" may refer to inconstancies the lovers have endured.

The third stanza introduces a more abstract metaphor, linking religion and nature. This "Sea of Faith" reveals the speaker's loss of belief and his disillusionment. With this negative example, Arnold contrasts the once "bright girdle furled with full faith" and the now "melancholy, drear, and naked" beaches swept by the "breath of night wind." This analogy seems developed to elicit both empathy and response on the part of his beloved. He has lost everything—God and Nature, but she can be his salvation because, by implication, he still believes in her. She will be his faith, his light, his constant sea.

As the poem reaches its climax, the speaker again moves from the general to the specific. He returns to the present and implores his beloved to accept his fervent plea: "Ah, love, let us be true to one another!" Arnold emphasizes this assertion by contrasting it with the concluding lines of the poem. Only this line is a simple direct imperative. The rest of the stanza is a complex set of similes that reiterate the major points of the speaker's argument.

In the first stanza, the couple was literally on the land, but, now, the world is "like a land of dreams." Repetition reinforces what the dream may be: "so various, so beautiful, so new." Immediately, this line is contrasted with a negative series focusing not on the dream, but on the reality: "neither joy, nor love, nor light, nor certitude, nor peace, nor help for pain." The final simile, "as on a darkling plain, where ignorant armies clash by night," is a direct contrast to the first stanza's softly lit sea, solitude, and serenity. Arnold puts the final touch on his argument by implying that they, the lovers who are true, therefore, must be everything positive and enlightened because they are in sharp contrast to the images and techniques presented throughout the poem.

Analysis of the Body of the Essay

topic sentence Drawing his images from nature, Arnold creates a romantic scene that will be contrasted in the final stanza. As he implores his love to look from the window at the world beneath them, the poet introduces the sea and the land, and the diction positions them as the dominant contradictory symbols of the poem. Although it is night, "moon, fair, light, gleams, and **reference** glimmering" all illuminate the "calm, full, and tranquil bay." And yet, in his description of **reference** the "sweet night," Arnold includes the word, "only" to imply something other than the idyllic **reference** vision. This change in mood is meant to make his beloved uneasy, so she will be receptive to **connection to thesis** him later when he proposes an antidote to the ensuing negative examples.

To further his position, Arnold juxtaposes the sea and the "moon-blanched land", light and dark, and seeing and hearing. Now he orders his love to "Listen!" as well as look. This **reference** imperative is also for the reader, and we can hear, through onomatopoeia, the "grating roar" of the pebbles breaking the quiet tone. The following lines, 10–14, depend on sound devices **reference** and punctuation to develop contrast. A succession of caesuras breaks the iambic meter and **example** makes the speaker/reader start and stop and start again, much like the rhythm of the waves **example** themselves which "begin, and cease, and then again, begin." Perhaps, Arnold is using this pattern as a parallel to the lovers' relationship. It, too, may have its high and low tides.

topic sentence Allusions to Sophocles and the Aegean allow Arnold to move from the immediate and specific images of the first stanza to a more general argument. Like the eternal sea, human **universal idea** misery is a common experience, and this example from the past will make his argument for loyalty and love more poignant and universal. His diction now is negative; the sea is "turbid, **reference** distant and northern." It is possible his love has also been remote and cold. Again, one can **connection to thesis** infer that the "ebb and flow" may refer to inconstancies the lovers have endured.

topic sentence The third stanza introduces a more abstract metaphor, linking religion and nature. This **interpretation** "Sea of Faith" reveals the speaker's loss of belief and his disillusionment. With this negative **reference** example, Arnold contrasts the once "bright girdle furled with full faith" and the now **reference** "melancholy, drear, and naked" beaches swept by the "breath of night wind." This analogy seems developed to elicit both empathy and response on the part of his beloved. He has lost everything—God and Nature, but she can be his salvation because, by implication, he still **interpretation** believes in her. She will be his faith, his light, his constant sea.

topic sentence As the poem reaches its climax, the speaker again moves from the general to the specific. **reference** He returns to the present and implores his beloved to accept his fervent plea: "Ah, love, let us be true to one another!" Arnold emphasizes this assertion by <u>contrasting</u> it with the concluding lines of the poem. Only this line is a simple direct imperative. The rest of the stanza is a complex set of similes which reiterate the major points of the speaker's argument.

example In the first stanza, the couple was literally on the land, but, now, the world is "like a land of dreams." <u>Repetition</u> reinforces what the dream may be: "so various, so beautiful, so new."

example Immediately, this line is <u>contrasted</u> with a negative series focusing not on the dream, but on the reality: "neither joy, nor love, nor light, nor certitude, nor peace, nor help for pain."

example The final <u>simile</u>, "as on a darkling plain, where ignorant armies clash by night," is a direct <u>contrast</u> to the first stanza's softly lit sea, solitude, and serenity. <u>Arnold puts the final touch on his argument by implying that they, the lovers who are true, therefore, must be everything</u>

topic <u>positive and enlightened because they are in sharp opposition to the images and techniques</u>

sentence <u>presented throughout the poem.</u>

Comments

Obviously the writer of this essay has a clear understanding of the prompt and the poem. The paper is well focused, strongly based on the text, and clearly expressed. Specific references are appropriate and smoothly integrated into the essay. Topic adherence is reinforced throughout by echo words and connective tissue.

The essay's thesis, that the poem is developed by contrast to persuade the lover to her partner's viewpoint, is reiterated in each paragraph. The words, *contrast, contradictory,* and *opposition* are used to maintain this thread. Similarly, *argument, persuade, convince, point of view, position,* and *assertion* all focus the paper on its topic: the poem as an argument for reciprocal love. The illustrations of diction, meter, organization, metaphor, and similes relate the meaning of the poem and the essay directly to the prompt.

References to *now* and *then, again, first* and *last stanza, beginning, climax* and *concludes* serve as transitions to link and move the sections of the essay.

The level and thoroughness of analysis is the strength of the essay. The writer moves beyond the average paper by drawing a parallel between the movement of the lines and meter and the movement of the waves. This technical information is then carried over to the interpretive level with the insight that the ebb and flow of the sea might refer to the pattern of the relationship. The understanding and explanation of the use of contrast as a persuasive tool is also an upper level concept. The writer understands Arnold's real motivation for the poem and is aware of the emotional manipulation occurring. Including inferences shows the readers of the essay the depth of the writer's interpretive skills. The vocabulary, such as *juxtapose, idyllic, romantic, onomatopoeia, implication,* is used appropriately and also raises the level of the essay. Likewise, the sentence variety enhances the readability level.

The essay itself follows the pattern of the poem, and this approach maintains clarity. In addition, it opens and closes with direct references to the text that serve to unify the paper. The presentation is on task and accessible, reflecting good planning and prewriting efforts.

Student Samples

The transitions are bracketed for you.

Student A

["The Passionate Shepherd to His Love"] *is very idyllic, flowery even. Marlowe uses words like "pleasures," "melodious," and "pretty lambs," for their connotative enhancements to the romantic tone of the poem. The line "And a thousand fragrant posies" is particularly powerful with its over-the-top image of a sea of flowers: "fragrant" with its hint of elegance, beauty, and grace, and "posies" reinforcing that image of soft, delicate, and perhaps gently swaying fields in which to frolic. The complete poetic mosaic, thus, creates a field of brightest colors, with the scent of sweet perfume and lazy bees droning overhead in this most romantic of rainbow paradises.*

[The second poem is the cynical twin of the first.] *Here, all the high-minded and romantic ideals are dashed into the "rocks grow[n] cold." Line by line, stanza by stanza, Sir Walter Raleigh's "The Nymph's Reply to the Shepherd" opposes the romantic attitude of the passionate shepherd of the first poem. The reply is: no, poor shepherd, you are a dreamer. "Cold," "gall," "fade," and "wither" are all chillingly clipped answers to the shepherd's lovesick plea. He would wither away, longing for the immortal nymph. Here, the poet presents a realistic (if somewhat pessimistic) viewpoint on life and love. The shepherd and the nymph become a metaphor for life and how nothing lasts forever; thus, everything is in vain.*

[This negative metaphor] *is developed by Raleigh's use of nonflowery, realistic diction. For example, "Soon break, soon wither, soon forgotten" is a far cry from the "posies" and fair lined slippers" of the first poem. The nymph's reply is cold and harsh with heart-breaking negative connotations for the shepherd and others who read the poem. Romanticism is challenged, calling to light the follies of the optimistic and pining fantasies of Christopher Marlowe's poem.*

Comments

This successful contrast/comparison essay presents a thorough and well-organized series of points. They are substantiated by text and insightful interpretation. This student writer:

- demonstrates a thorough understanding of the prompt and its demands;
- clearly illustrates the differing attitudes toward life presented in the two poems;
- effectively develops comparison and contrast points;
- makes appropriate and meaningful references to the texts to support the analysis;
- uses inferences to draw conclusions about the underlying meaning of the poems;
- demonstrates strong topic adherence;
- employs a mature writing style.

Student B

[From the very beginning,] *the specific tone of praise and empathy are established. The author's choice of words praises Paret and looks at him and at his fighting style with a sense of awe. Descriptive phrases such as, "that he had an unusual ability to take a punch;" or that "he took three punches to the head in order to give back two."*

begin to lead an already shocked reader toward the inevitable ending. When Mailer uses the words "bouncing," "headache," and "bad maulings," an image of an animal springing from a fight pop into mind. However, <u>this</u> animal doesn't know when to give up, that is why he doesn't lose a fight; he just receives bad punches or beatings. Because of details and diction like these, the reader knows this man Benny Paret was special and would not give up, no matter what.

As one begins to read the second paragraph, the tone changes slightly. Paret is still proud; however, his showmanship is faltering. This, in turn, leads to his demise which is unlike any other. Much like his entire boxing career, Paret's death was brutal, but respectable. The first seven sentences in the second paragraph set the reader up for the climax. They detail the Kid's "first sign of weakness," and "inspired particular shame," allowing the reader to see that, as Mailer states, "Paret began to wilt." For the first time the crowd sees him as human, a man, a man about to take the last beating of his life.

When the writer begins to narrate the actual mauling, or should I say killing, he goes into gory animalistic detail, comparing Paret to a "huge boxed rat" and Griffith to a "cat ready to rip the life out . . ." Right away, the reader begins to imagine this poor fighter trapped in the corner and this ogre beating away at him. Later on, Griffith's punches are compared to a "piston rod which has broken through the crankcase;" and to "a baseball bat demolishing a pumpkin," the pumpkin being Paret's head. All of a sudden, the reader not only visualizes this murder but hears the sounds that go with it, the sound of "goosh" or "whoosh," two sounds that aren't very pleasant when talking about a human being's head. Describing the force needed to pull Griffith away, Mailer talks about his uncontrollable power, much like a rabid animal in real life, one with no feelings, just waiting to win. Griffith is portrayed as a man with no remorse.

The last paragraph really hits home, making the reader say, "Wow" or "Oh, my G-d." The idea of Paret dying on his feet, and the impact left on the crowd is almost overpowering. When Mailer chooses the word "hover" a certain heavy feeling just kind of hangs with the reader. The Kid's death is slow and admirable. The metaphor "sank slowly" like a "large ship which turns . . ." gives a feeling of respect, the kind we give to great ships that sink at sea. In the last sentence, "the sound of Griffith's . . . chopping into a wet log," brutally drives home and reminds the reader of the relentless beating Paret sustained before he died.

Comments

The body of this student essay indicates a writer who understood both Mailer's text and how to analyze the rhetorical strategies used by the author. This sample is a good model of an essay that smoothly integrates details and specific references into both the sentence and the paragraph.

Paragraph 1 points out Mailer's use of descriptive words and phrases, cites specific examples, AND comments about the purpose and effect of these citations. Paragraph 2 provides an example of another form of citation. Here the writer refers to WHERE in the text the reference occurs. Note also how smoothly the details are integrated into the sentences. In paragraph 3, specific references are linked to the student writer's main points, and he correctly makes use of the ellipsis. The final body paragraph also uses the ellipsis correctly and well when the writer pulls out just the phrases of a metaphor he needs to make a point. And, don't forget to take note of the sequential transitional phrases we've blocked for you.

Workout 1

Go to your current writing portfolio or folder and choose one of your essays to examine closely.

1. The title of the essay is _____.

2. The subject of the essay is _____

_____.

3. The purpose is _____.

4. The audience is _____.

5. My thesis statement is located in paragraph _____. It is

_____

_____

_____

6. I have _____ major points in this essay. They are:

_____   _____

_____   _____

_____   _____

7. I've used the following organization method(s) to develop my points. (Check all that apply)

_____ Chronological order

_____ Spatial order

_____ Subject by subject

_____ Point by point examines

_____ Categorizing

_____ A single cause leading to a single effect or multiple effects

_____ Multiple causes leading to a single effect or multiple effects

_____ A single effect and the single or multiple cause(s)

_____ Multiple effects and the single or multiple cause(s)

_____ Most important to least important or vice versa

_____ Deduction

_____ Induction

8. My essay has _____ paragraphs.

9. The transitional elements in each of my paragraphs are:

¶ 2 _____

¶ 3 _____

¶ 4 _____

¶ 5 _____

¶ 6 _____

¶ 7 _____

¶ 8 _____

¶ 9 _____

¶ 10 _____

10. Each of my paragraphs has a topic sentence. _____ yes _____ no

11. Each of my body paragraphs has specific examples, references, etc., to support both my thesis and the topic sentence. _____ yes _____ no

12. I've made certain to avoid just listing examples, references, etc., _____ yes _____ no

13. I've connected each of my examples, or references, or points to the subject of my essay. _____ yes _____ no

14. If I had the opportunity to rewrite any of the body paragraphs of this essay, I would choose to rewrite paragraph _____ because _____
_____.

15. Here's my revision: _____

_____

_____

_____

_____

_____

_____

_____

_____

_____

_____

We strongly urge you to work through this and other writing and revising activities with members of your English class or members of your peer reading group. Having other readers provide you with feedback and vice versa is vital for strengthening your writing skills.

Supporting Syntax

Remember that part of your responsibility as a writer is clarity, whether you're composing the opening of your essay, the body, or its conclusion. As writing trainers, we can tell you that there are particular syntax problems that you should be aware of and that you should try to avoid if you want to ensure this clarity. Consider the following three topics.

Incorporating Quotations and References from the Text into a Sentence

There are several techniques that allow you to place a specific textual reference in the sentence:

- The reference to the speaker or writer or character; for example, *According to Mark Twain* . . .
- Citing the location of the reference; for example, lines 3–5 of paragraph 2 pose a rhetorical question.
- Placing the reference inside the sentence to illustrate a point; for example, *Dickens's diction such as "somber," "wasted," and "suffocating" establishes the motif of illness and death.*
- A general reference; for example, *In the first part of the poem* . . .
- Beginning a sentence with a quotation; for example, *"But why you ask me, should this tale be told/to men grown old, or who are growing old?"* signals a transition in the poem.
- Splitting references; for example, *"An insurmountable precipice"* faces Hester in her quest for equality, and mustering courage, she is able to *"start back from a deep chasm."*
- AVOID THE LAUNDRY LIST. For example, There is frequent use of assonance in the poem, such as *"woe," "bemoan," "lone," and "o'er."* (This list is NOT linked to any meaning or point being made.) The solution: With such words as *"woe," "bemoan," "lone,"* and *"o'er,"* the poet's assonance approximates the sounds of someone lamenting.

> We recommend that you use a combination of the above techniques in any given essay. We also want to stress the importance of making certain that you link any and all of your references to a specific point you are making.

Using Transitions

Why worry about transitions? Simple. They constitute the primary connective tissue within the body of your essay. Transitions will:

- connect the various parts of the essay to both your thesis and to the preceding paragraph
- enable you to move from one thought to another without confusing your reader
- set up a sequence, if needed
- indicate cause and effect
- delineate the areas of contrast and comparison

Below is a brief listing of frequently used transitional words and phrases:

- Most often used and most "natural" transitions in sentences or brief sequences of sentences: *and, but, or, nor, for, yet*
- Some other commonly used transitions between paragraphs or sections of longer works:

  _____ (numerical) *first, second, third, primarily,* etc.
  _____ (sequential) *then, finally, next*
  _____ (additional) *furthermore, moreover, again, also, similarly*
  _____ (illustrative) *for example, for instance, to illustrate*
  _____ (contrast, comparison, alternative) *on the other hand, nevertheless, conversely, instead, however, still*

_____ (cause and effect) *therefore, consequently, as a result, accordingly*

_____ (affirmation) *of course, obviously, indeed*

Active and Passive Voice

You've probably heard this more often than you can remember—"Avoid the passive voice." And, most of the time, you've ignored this piece of advice or used the passive voice without realizing it. Well, we're asking you NOT to ignore it and NOT to use if at all possible. Nothing can add a deadening quality to your writing than passive voice.

We know; we know; you want to sound as "intelligent" as you possibly can, and using long, involved sentences with multisyllabic words that only a thesaurus could love is the way to do it. WRONG! Knowing your material and presenting it clearly is your best bet.

Just what is active and passive voice?

To answer this question, look at the following sentences:

The ball was driven by Paul.

1. What is the subject? _____

2. What is the verb tense? _____

3. Is the verb simple or compound? _____

4. What is the prepositional phrase? _____

5. How many words are in the sentence? _____

Paul drove the car.

1. What is the subject? _____

2. What is the verb tense? _____

3. Is the verb simple or compound? _____

4. Is there a prepositional phrase? _____

5. How many words are in the sentence? _____

Which of the two sentences has the subject of the sentence doing the action? _____

Which one has the subject being acted upon? _____

When the writing lets the reader know that the subject is **doing the acting**, you have **active voice**. When the subject is acted upon or is the goal of the action, and, therefore, NOT responsible, you have **Passive Voice**.

With this in mind, identify which of the two sentences above is active and which one is passive. Without a doubt, we know you chose the second as active and the first as passive.

Here's another example:

The new free trade agreement was signed last night.

Who signed the treaty? Who do we blame if the agreement falters? We don't know, do we? Passive voice avoids responsibility. It is a primary tool of those who wish to obfuscate or those who lack confidence and decisiveness.

Why not give the true picture and write:

> *Last night, the President of the United States and the President of Mexico signed a new free trade agreement.*

More "Avoiders"

There are two AP English "idiosyncrasies" we would like to see every student avoid.

1. Avoid this type of phrase: *Poe uses diction . . .*

A writer doesn't *use* diction. His or her word choice is *categorized* as diction. Therefore, the proper phrasing would be: *Poe's diction . . .*

2. Avoid the judgmental qualifiers; for example, "Wordsworth's *masterful* use of the English language. . . "; "The *magnificent* argument . . ."

Masterful and *magnificent* are qualifiers. You may be at a later date, but at this point in your academic career, you are NOT in a position to make this type of judgment. They are just empty fillers and do nothing to enhance your essay.

The solution: *Wordsworth's use of language . . .*
   This argument . . .

CHAPTER ▶ 10

Writing the Conclusion of the Essay and Revising

IN THIS CHAPTER

Summary: Refine strategies for effectively concluding the essay

Key Ideas
- ✪ Practice with a variety of concluding techniques
- ✪ Examine student samples and commentary
- ✪ Practice with your own writing
- ✪ Master a method for revision

KEY IDEA

"Leave 'em wantin' more." That's a piece of advice most performers are given early in their career. We'd like to give you a similar, yet somewhat different, piece of advice. "Leave 'em feelin' satisfied." You've made an assertion and provided support for that assertion in the body of your essay. And, you want the reader to leave your presentation understanding your point of view and accepting your evidence in support of it. You also want your reader to sense a kind of closure and not feel as if left swinging in the breeze. The obvious way to provide this sense of security and closure is to compose an appropriate conclusion.

The old, tried-and-true conclusion is the all too familiar one. It usually begins with "In summary," or "In conclusion," or "Finally" followed by a review of the thesis and major points made in the presentation. Although this might be useful in an extended and complex essay, it is not needed, nor is it recommended, for a 500–1000-word presentation in a response to a college-level writing prompt, whether timed or untimed.

"Writing is easy. All you have to do is sit down in front of the computer and open a vein."
—Red Smith

With that in mind, you no doubt are asking yourself, "Okay, if not a summary, what should I write?" You could try one of the following:

- Link your conclusion to something you said in the introduction.
- Link your idea to a more universal point.
- Relate a personal experience or idea to your thesis.
- Link your thesis to the world of your reader.
- Challenge your reader.
- End with a rhetorical question or imperative statement.
- Use an anecdote to reinforce a major point in your essay.
- End with an important line from the original text.

Your conclusion should leave the reader with a sense of you as a person with a voice and a valid, interesting point of view. This is your last chance to make an impression. Don't lose the opportunity. Consider the following samples from students' essays.

Sample Conclusions

AP English Language
"A Presidential Candidate"

Throughout "A Presidential Candidate," Mark Twain focuses on his negative qualities rather than on the good, which is the usual MO for a political candidate. He enumerates absurdly opposite positions to the usual campaign promises. I only wish every candidate for political office could read this parody. As a matter of fact, I think I will e-mail this to all my representatives who hold national, state, and local offices. Thanks, Mr. Twain.

Comments

This conclusion links the final remarks to the more universal point of current politicians needing to reconsider their own approaches to addressing the electorate. The conclusion ends with a personal challenge that the writer makes to himself.

AP English Literature
Sample Conclusion from the "Dover Beach" Prompt

"Ah, love, let us be true," pleads the speaker and we can imagine the lovers, just the two of them, together, in the present, against the dark past and unknown future.

Comments

Highlighting the most important line of the poem, this conclusion succinctly summarizes the essential contrasts presented in the introduction to the essay.

Student Samples

Student A

Throughout history, the rich and famous have enjoyed privileges that the common man hasn't

been allowed. Many current headline stories reveal the depth to which money and fame can infect the justice system. Meanwhile, those clothed in "rags" continue to get shafted by a system that they do not influence nor control.

Comments

This conclusion aggressively finalizes the writer's position. With no rehashing of the prompt and no repetition of the thesis, this student leaves his reader with an implied challenge—do you dare to agree or disagree with me?

Student B

In any case, that's what it comes down to. The Calvinists believed that wealth was a sign from God that a man had been pre-selected to reside in heaven. So, our wealthy folks are really heaven-sent. Perfect angels don't need laws anyway, right?

Comments

Using a sarcastic rhetorical question to end this essay is a thought-provoking way for this student writer to make his or her own voice and point of view heard loudly and clearly.

Workout 1

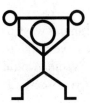

You're going to be examining the same three essays you've been working with in Chapters 7 and 8 to complete this exercise set.

1. For each of the conclusions cite the transitional element that connects the ending to the body of the essay.

   Essay #1: _____

   Essay #2: _____

   Essay #3: _____

2. What technique(s) did you use to create each of your conclusions?

Essay			*Technique*
1 _____	2 _____	3 _____	Link your conclusion to something you said in the introduction.
1 _____	2 _____	3 _____	Link your idea to a more universal point.
1 _____	2 _____	3 _____	Relate a personal experience or idea to your thesis.
1 _____	2 _____	3 _____	Link your thesis to the world of your reader.
1 _____	2 _____	3 _____	Challenge your reader.
1 _____	2 _____	3 _____	End with a rhetorical question or imperative statement.
1 _____	2 _____	3 _____	Use an anecdote to reinforce a major point in your essay.
1 _____	2 _____	3 _____	Use a quotation from the original text.

3. Have you avoided "In summary," "In conclusion," etc., in each of your conclusions?

   1 ____ yes ____ no; 2 ____ yes ____ no; 3 ____ yes ____ no

4. Select one of your three conclusions and rewrite it using TWO different techniques.

5. I chose the conclusion to essay _____ 1 _____ 2 _____ 3.

6. For the conclusion to essay _____ I've decided to use the following techniques:

    Technique 1: _____

    Technique 2: _____

7. On a separate sheet of paper rewrite the conclusion using the two different techniques.

8. Of the three different conclusions, including my original, to essay _____, the one

    I like best is _____ the original _____ the conclusion using technique 1

    _____ the conclusion using technique 2.

9. I think my choice is the best conclusion because _____

    _____

    _____ .

Revision

The process you just completed is a type of revision. But, this is just one of many ways to go about reworking your essay. To give you an idea of some of these methods, we'd like to examine the real work of revision. To examine the real work of revision (and, as some would say, the real work of writing), we are going to provide you with several different methods that you could employ to revise your essays.

A Very Simple Method

This is a quick overview that you can do alone or with a peer reader. You should consider and take notes, where and when necessary, as you consider each of the following.

RECONSIDER YOUR OPENING PARAGRAPH.

1. Is there a clear thesis statement?
2. Does it somehow grab the interest of your reader?
3. In what tense are you going to present your ideas?

ORGANIZATION

1. What is the purpose of your essay?
2. What rhetorical strategies, techniques and devices do you use to achieve this purpose?
3. Is your essay presented as formal or informal?
4. Are there transitional words/phrases connecting the body paragraphs to each other?
5. Do you have an ending that naturally evolves from your essay?

SYNTAX

1. Are all verbs in the same tense? Is there a reason for any verb to be a different tense?
2. Do all words/phrases adhere to the essay being formal or informal?
3. Does *each* pronoun have a *clear* antecedent?
4. Is there a clear reason for every comma used in the essay?

5. Examine the beginning of each sentence. Is there an overuse of a type of opening? If there is, work on changing some to achieve variety.

6. Do you have a variety of sentence types? Simple? Compound? Complex? Compound–complex?

A More Involved Revision Method That Can Provide Valuable Feedback.

1. What is the subject of your essay?

2. What do you hope your reader will come away with after having read your essay?

3. With the answers to the above questions in mind, what is the thesis statement? Quote it exactly.

4. How have you ordered the development of the support for your claim? Is it in chronological order, spatial, least important to most important, etc.? List the major points in your essay in the order that each appears.

5. Do each of your paragraphs, other than the first, have a transitional word or phrase? List them:

PARAGRAPH #	TRANSITION WORD/PHRASE
2	
3	
4	
5	
6	
7	
8	
9	
10	

6. Take a really close look at your introductory paragraph(s). Is it made very clear to your reader what the subject of this essay is? Does it contain the thesis/claim? Does the last sentence of the introduction lead easily to the next section of your essay?

7. Take a close look at your conclusion. Does it bring closure to your essay in such a way that your reader should feel he or she knows your point of view, attitude, and why he or she should care about it?

8. Let's call this next part of the revising process **Coap**ing.

   Cut: bracket all the best or most workable sentences and cut out everything else.

   Order: put these pieces in the best order, decide what your main point is; put in transitions.

   Add: do any additional writing that is needed.

   Polish: make the sentences smooth and readable.
   - Cut unnecessary words and phrases
   - Clarify anything that isn't clear.
   - Combine any sentences that lend themselves to combining, for greater flow and variety.
   - Correct typos, spelling, punctuation, and grammar.

9. And last, but most important, **read your essay out loud to someone, and someone must read it out loud to you**. (Do this for your first draft and all other drafts.)

10. As a result of this reading aloud, have you located any major errors that need to be revised? If so, list them.

A Revision Method for a Writing Assignment Related to Literary Texts

1. The text(s) I am working with is/are _____.

2. My essay is _____ formal _____ informal.

3. The thesis/claim of my essay is _____.

4. I have made certain to include the title(s) and author(s) of my texts. They are _____

_____.

5. The main rhetorical strategy I used to develop my essay is

_____ contrast/comparison, _____ exposition,
_____ definition, _____ cause/effect, _____ process,
_____ classification, _____ analysis, _____ description.

7. I have also made use of the following:

_____ contrast/comparison, _____ examples,
_____ definition, _____ cause/effect, _____ process,
_____ classification, _____ analysis, _____ description.

8. I organized my essay around _____ character relationships, _____ conflicts,

_____ significance of setting, _____ the writer's use of symbols,

_____ the writer's manipulation of his/her point of view, _____ the development of imagery.

9. I have made _____ specific references to my first text, _____ and

_____ specific references to my second text, _____.

10. When referring to printed text, each one of my references cites the appropriate **line**, **paragraph**, **stanza**, or **page**, depending on whether it is prose or poetry. Here are my references:

Reference #	Page #	Paragraph #	Line #	Stanza #
_____	_____	_____	_____	_____
_____	_____	_____	_____	_____
_____	_____	_____	_____	_____

11. Below are the transition words/phrases I use between paragraphs.

PARAGRAPH #	TRANSITION WORD/PHRASE
2	
3	
4	
5	

6

7

8

9

10

12. My ending makes a final statement rather than summarizing what I've already said.

_____ Yes _____ No

Sample Essays

Essay in Response to the Prompt for Mark Twain's "A Presidential Candidate"

We've all heard the following before, haven't we? "Trust me. I only want to be your public servant. I will always work for the common good of all." It's so familiar and so shallow that the political cynic in each of us responds, "<u>Sure</u> we should. <u>Sure</u> he does. <u>Sure</u> he will." Aware of this cynicism, Mark Twain plays with our political suspicions in "A Presidential Candidate," a parody of the typical campaign speech.

Informal diction contributes to the overall humor of this parody. Most of us expect a modicum of seriousness and dignity from our political candidates. And, we expect this to be evident in their speeches and writing. To the contrary, Twain uses "folksy" and regional words and phrases throughout the essay. In paragraph one, avoiding lofty language, the author writes "pretty much made up my mind" to tell his audience that he has made a decision, and he invites congressional scrutiny with "let it prowl." Paragraph two has Twain's grandfather "bowling up" a tree when he is chased from his house by the narrator. And, in his final paragraph, the author uses his own method to appeal to the common man when says, "If my country don't want me . . ."

Exaggeration also plays a major role in the creation of this humorous takeoff on campaign speeches. The anecdote about the author and his grandfather is in every way over the top. Treeing and shooting his grandfather with buckshot is both ludicrous and highly improbable. The absurdity continues in paragraph four with the tale of his burying his dead aunt "under my grapevine." In paragraph five, Twain takes a wide and caustic swing at political candidates who promise to stand up for the common man. He says, ". . . I regard the poor man, in his present condition, as so much wasted raw material." The author's outrageous suggestion to kill and cannibalize "the poor workingman . . ." and ". . . stuff him into sausages," would have made Jonathan Swift very proud.

Almost all of Twain's selection of details contributes to the irony of this piece. We expect heroic tales of the candidate's war experiences, but this candidate describes and admits his cowardice in the face of battle, even while making a tongue-in-cheek reference to Washington. Instead of claiming to be a financial virgin, as most candidates do, Twain readily characterizes himself as money hungry and willing to get it any way he can. Adding to the irony that is the basis for the announcement, Twain makes references to the U.S. Constitution and asks rhetorical questions about both his fitness for the presidency and his being a "victim of absurd prejudices."

Throughout "A Presidential Candidate," Mark Twain focuses on his negative qualities rather than on the positive which is the usual MO for a political candidate. He enumerates absurdly opposite positions to the usual campaign promises. I only wish every candidate for political office could read this parody. As a matter of fact, I think I will e-mail this to all my representatives who hold national, state, and local offices. Thanks, Mr. Twain.

Essay in Response to the Prompt for "Dover Beach"

From "calm to clash, from light to darkling, from sea to land," Matthew Arnold's poem, "Dover Beach" is a study in contrast. This contrast, developed throughout the poem by a progression of increasingly negative examples, is necessary to convince his love to be true. In addition, poetic devices and techniques enable Arnold to encourage his love to see the urgency of his desire and passion. Metaphors, allusions, organization, and appeals to the senses reinforce his argument, that love and lovemaking are the only things of certainty in an ignorant and hostile world.

This contrast is a subtle way to persuade his love to his point of view. By gradually leading her to realize that life is, and always has been, filled with "misery and uncertainty," he establishes his argument that only their commitment to one another can counteract the inevitable struggle and disillusionment of life.

Drawing his images from nature, Arnold creates a romantic scene that will later be contrasted in the final stanza. As he implores his love to look from the window at the world beneath them, the poet introduces the sea and the land, and the diction positions them as the dominant contradictory symbols of the poem. Although it is night, "moon, fair, light, gleams, and glimmering" all illuminate the "calm, full, and tranquil bay." And yet, in his description of the " sweet night," Arnold includes the word, "only" to imply something other than the idyllic vision. This change in mood is meant to make his beloved uneasy, so she will be receptive to him later when he proposes an antidote to the ensuing negative examples.

To further his position, Arnold juxtaposes the sea and the "moon-blanched land," light and dark, and seeing and hearing. Now he orders his love to "Listen!" as well as look. This imperative is also for the reader, and we can hear, through onomatopoeia, the "grating roar" of the pebbles breaking the quiet tone. The following lines, 10–14, depend on sound devices and punctuation to develop contrast. A succession of caesuras breaks the iambic meter and makes the speaker and reader start and stop and start again, much like the rhythm of the waves themselves, which "begin, and cease, and then again, begin." Perhaps, Arnold is using this pattern as a parallel to the lovers' relationship. It, too, may have its high and low tides.

Allusions to Sophocles and the Aegean allow Arnold to move from the immediate and specific images of the first stanza to a more general argument. Like the eternal sea, human misery is a common experience, and this example from the past will make his argument for loyalty and love more poignant and universal. His diction now is negative; the sea is "turbid, distant and northern." It is possible his love has also been remote and cold. Again, one can infer that the "ebb and flow" may refer to inconstancies the lovers have endured.

The third stanza introduces a more abstract metaphor, linking religion and nature. This "Sea of Faith" reveals the speaker's loss of belief and his disillusionment. With this negative example, Arnold contrasts the once "bright girdle furled with full faith" and the now "melancholy, drear, and naked" beaches swept by the "breath of night wind." This analogy seems developed to elicit both empathy and response on the part of his beloved. He has lost everything—God and Nature, but she can be his salvation because, by implication, he still believes in her. She will be his faith, his light, his constant sea.

As the poem reaches its climax, the speaker again moves from the general to the specific. He returns to the present and implores his beloved to accept his fervent plea: "Ah, love, let us be true to one another!" Arnold emphasizes this assertion by contrasting it with the concluding lines of the poem. Only this line is a simple direct imperative. The rest of the stanza is a complex set of similes that reiterate the major points of the speaker's argument.

In the first stanza, the couple was literally on the land, but, now, the world is "like a land of dreams." Repetition reinforces what the dream may be: "so various, so beautiful, so new." Immediately, this line is contrasted with a negative series focusing not on the dream, but on the reality: "neither joy, nor love, nor light, nor certitude, nor peace, nor help for pain." The final simile, "as on a darkling plain, where ignorant armies clash by night," is a direct contrast to the first stanza's softly lit sea, solitude, and serenity. Arnold puts the final touch on his argument by implying that they, the lovers who are true, therefore, must be everything positive and enlightened because they are in sharp contrast to the negative images and techniques presented throughout the poem.

"Ah, love, let us be true," pleads the speaker, and we can imagine the lovers, just the two of them, together, in the present, against the dark past and unknown future.

STEP 5

Build Your Test-taking Confidence

CHAPTER 11

Practice with Sample AP English Language Exam Essays

IN THIS CHAPTER

Summary: Apply what you've learned thus far to sample AP English Language prompts and essays

KEY IDEA

Key Ideas
✪ Pull it all together
✪ Consider the rubrics as guidelines
✪ Read and assess actual student essays
✪ Encounter and interact with a synthesis essay prompt

"A deadline is negative inspiration. Still, it's better than no inspiration at all."
—Rita Mae Brown

STRATEGY

And nothing can give you writing "inspiration" more quickly than an AP essay prompt in a timed situation. If you've been diligent and persevered throughout your writing training program, you're ready for this experience. You can do it. As your writing trainers we have a few last words of advice for you.

- Read the prompt thoroughly and carefully. Deconstruct it the way you practiced earlier in this book.
- If there is a given text, read and notate it as we did in Chapter 6.
- Organize your notes and write the thesis statement as you have practiced.
- Write the essay with the prompt, purpose, and thesis statement always uppermost in your mind.
- Make certain to include specific examples and/or references related to the thesis.

- Incorporate your examples and references into the paragraphs.
- Be sure to provide adequate and appropriate attribution.
- Allow yourself a couple of minutes to proofread your essay quickly. Check for syntax, topic adherence, and coherence. If you have to eliminate something, *neatly* draw a line through it. (Better a cross out than a blatant error.) If you have to add something, depending on the length and location, use the carat ∧, or parenthesis ( ), or asterisk *.

Sample AP English Language Essay Prompt 1

In "At the Funeral" from *An Unfinished Burlesque of Books on Etiquette*, Mark Twain addresses the social norms surrounding a very serious subject. In a well-written essay, identify Twain's purpose and analyze the rhetorical strategies he uses to develop and support this purpose.

"At the Funeral"

Do not criticize the person in whose honor the entertainment is given.

Make no remarks about his equipment. If the handles [of the encasement] are plated, it is best to not observe it.

If the odor of the flowers is too oppressive for your comfort, remember that they were not brought there for you, and that the person for whom they were brought suffers no inconvenience from their presence.   5

Listen, with an intense expression of attention as you can command, to the official statement of the character and history of the person in whose honor the entertainment is given; and if these statistics should seem to fail to tally with the facts in places, do not nudge your neighbor, or press your foot upon his toes, or manifest,   10
by any other sign, your awareness that taffy is being distributed.

If the official hopes expressed concerning the person in whose honor the entertainment is given are known to you to be oversized, let it pass – do not interrupt.

At the moving passages, be moved – but only according to the degree of your intimacy with the parties giving the entertainment, or with the party in whose honor the   15
entertainment is given. Where a blood relation sobs, an intimate friend should choke up, a distant acquaintance should sigh, a stranger should merely fumble sympathetically with his handkerchief. Where the occasion is military, the emotions should be graded according to military rank, the highest officer present taking precedence in emotional violence, and the rest modifying their feelings according to their position in the service.   20

Do not bring your dog.

Rubrics for Prompt 1
The High-Range Essay:

- Correctly identifies Twain's purpose and attitude toward his subject
- Effectively discusses/analyzes methods used to create the tone, attitude
- Effectively analyzes devices used to develop the purpose
- Effectively connects the humor to the author's purpose
- Recognizes and discusses the subtleties of the passage
- Good use of connective tissue

- Effectively manipulates language
- Clear organization and topic adherence
- Few, if any, syntactical errors

The Mid-Range Essay:

- Correctly identifies the author's purpose and attitude
- Adequately recognizes and analyzes the devices used to create tone and attitude
- Adequately analyzes the devices used to develop the purpose
- Recognition of Twain's subtleties may be missing
- Development not as strong/complete as the high range essays
- A few syntactical errors

The Low-Range Essay:

- Inadequate response to the prompt
- May misrepresent or incorrectly identify the author's purpose and attitude toward his subject
- May inaccurately identify and/or analyze rhetorical devices
- Ideas are incompletely developed
- Indicates a lack of control of diction, syntax and/or organization

Sample Student Essays

Student A

Do not pick your nose and lick your fingers while conversing with your dentist. Do not yell out instructions to actors in crowded movie theaters. If you sleep in the nude, always wear a long, heavy bathrobe when collecting your morning paper.

All of these instructions are rather obvious, I hope – but extremely humorous. I never realized Mark twain had such a great sense of humor. He makes a funeral, that ordinarily is a remarkably somber occasion, almost bearable with his sarcastic tone. I remember thinking that Tom Sawyer's own funeral in Twain's novel of the same name was amusing, but not quite as funny as "At the Funeral."

Because of the diction and syntax in this passage, the excerpt could easily qualify as a "Miss Manners" column from my local newspaper. It could also fit in with stuffy old British books. The very proper and elegant English used helps to make this piece so ironic. One would expect important matters to be discussed when "the official statement of the character and history of the person in whose honor" is read, but in actuality, one would be more likely to crack up with laughter. Who would even think about a mourner bringing a dog to a funeral, or examining the handles of the coffin to see if they are plated?

The things Twain suggests are too ridiculous for anyone to ever consider them as realistic possibilities, but that is exactly what makes this passage hilarious. This twist on such a serious event is positively unexpected, and at first glance, the reader is almost taken aback until he realizes that this is a humorous piece about a funeral. The fact that such a grave subject is touched upon in a jocular fashion is ironic. The whole work is based on irony and sarcasm. Twain provides a series of negative commandments, "do not nudge your neighbor," and "do not bring your dog!" This becomes more ridiculous as the passage progresses. Also, the tips Twain gives are so absurd that not one single person on the face of this planet would ever do any of the things Twain warns against.

My favorite part of "At the Funeral" is Twain counseling against showing one's acknowledgement of the truth that is being fudged (or the "taffy being distributed") when the person is being eulogized. It's so funny because people are supposed to be respectful at funerals, and this work is all about people being disrespectful.

The piece was enjoyable to read because it was so humorous. I would really like to read more of Mark Twain's work now that my eyes have been opened to his comedic side.

Student B

When many enter a funeral home, besides often being overcome with grief, many find themselves lost and wondering how to behave. Here, Mark Twain "conveniently forgets" the grief associated with funerals, and gives a humorous account of how one should act.

This passage's humorous tone, that is really sarcastic, reminds us of the first time each of us has entered a funeral home. I can remember my first time in one, wondering how to act or what to say. Twain's "guidelines" wouldn't have been of too much help to me before. But after attending a funeral it is a fresh reminder of what goes on, and of the thoughts that filled my head.

Twain uses short sentences and simple diction from the first line, making this a great essay you would find in a small chapter of a book or in an "upbeat" funeral home. At points the reader may think Twain is attempting to be serious, but by the end of the sentence, Twain uses the unexpected to create irony. Nowhere is this more obvious than when he tells us "Do not bring your dog!" at the end of the passage. Twists are placed in every sentence. Twain uses this every time that he states a thought that no refined person would ever say, such as referring to the "equipment." Paragraph four ends with an action many of us are guilty of at funeral homes. Many times I have heard untruths at funerals and have seen rude nudging.

Twain creates humor by expressing in words the thoughts people have inside at funeral homes. At every funeral I go to the smell of the flowers is always that same extreme smell. Do I comment to my family? Of course I don't. Here, Twain not only admits the "oppressive" nature of the flowers, but he acts sarcastically by telling of how the honored person cannot smell them.

Twain possessed a power to place the intangible feelings of many in words of meaning. He, like many, finds funerals confusing. Yet, he expresses the way he finds best to deal with some common feelings.

Rating the Student Essays
Student A
This is a high-range essay for the following reasons:

- Obviously understands the tone and intent of the passage
- Recognizes the devices used to create humor
- Presents a clear, controlled, confident voice
- Effectively addresses the requirements of the prompt
- Catches the subtleties of the passage
- Good connective tissue
- Mature diction and syntax
- Clear organization and topic coherence
- Few, if any, syntactical errors.

This writer attempts to recreate the tone and attitude of Twain's passage to indicate a true understanding of the prompt and selection. This risk indicates a confident student writer.

Student B

This is a mid-range essay for the following reasons:

- Correctly identifies Twain's tone and attitude
- Adequate illustration of the devices used to create and indicate tone and attitude
- Clear and concise analysis of the tone and attitude
- Needs to link observations with the text
- Obvious examples
- Not as subtle as the high-range essays
- Few, if any, lapses in diction and syntax

This solid, mid-range essay is developed by a writer who brings personal experience into the presentation. The essay's brevity and need of further development keep this student's response from being ranked in the higher range.

Sample AP English Language Essay Prompt 2

After carefully reading the following passage from Nathaniel Hawthorne's *The Scarlet Letter,* write a well-organized essay that analyzes how Hawthorne uses rhetorical strategies to explore and represent Hester Prynne's outlook on her own existence and that of women in general.

"Another View of Hester" (chapter XIII)

Indeed, the same dark question often rose into her mind with reference to the whole race of womanhood. Was existence worth accepting, even to the happiest among them? As concerned her own individual existence, she had long ago decided in the negative, and dismissed the point as settled. A tendency to speculation, though it may keep women quiet, as it does men, yet makes her sad. She discerns, it may be, such a hopeless task before her. As a first step, the whole system of society is to be torn down, and built up anew. Then, the very nature of the opposite sex, or its long hereditary trait, which has become like nature, is to be essentially modified, before women can be allowed to assume what seems a fair and suitable position. Finally, all other difficulties being obviated, a woman cannot take advantage of these preliminary reforms, until she herself shall have undergone a still mightier change; in which, perhaps, the ethereal essence, wherein she has her truest life, will be found to have evaporated. A woman never overcomes these problems by an exercise of thought. They are not to be solved, or only in one way. If her heart chance to come uppermost, they vanish. Thus, Hester Prynne, whose heart had lost its regular and healthy throb, wandered without a clew in the dark labyrinth of mind: now turned aside by an insurmountable precipice; now starting back from a deep chasm. There was a wild and ghastly scenery all around her, and a home and comfort nowhere. At times, a fearful doubt strove to possess her soul, whether it were better to send Pearl at once to heaven, and go herself to such futurity as Eternal Justice should provide.

The scarlet letter had not done its office.

Rubrics for Prompt 2

A High-Ranking Essay:

- Indicates a complete understanding of the prompt
- Clearly identifies and illustrates Hester's outlook on life
- Presents, describes, and analyzes various rhetorical strategies, devices, elements used by the author to create this outlook
- Effectively cites specific references from the text to illustrate and support points being made
- Is clear, well-organized, and coherent
- Demonstrates a mature writing style
- Contains minor errors/flaws, if any

Sample Student Essays

Student A

Before Title IX and the equal rights movement, most women were treated as inferior to men. As recent probes into Iraq and other middle Eastern nations have shown, they still are in large areas of the world. Women who have suffered and are suffering are often without a voice. It is hard to put into words the feeling of being inferior, as is the feeling of knowing you are being held down by invisible chains. Nathaniel Hawthorne, in his novel The Scarlet Letter, describes these feelings through the voice of Hester Prynne, the protagonist. In the passage, Hawthorne's diction, tone, and syntax help portray the plight of Prynne as a woman in hostile circumstances.

Hawthorne's diction is what sets the tone for the passage, and on a larger scale, the novel. In the first sentence he refers to the "dark question" that Prynne asked herself regarding her role as a woman. By injecting the word "dark," he immediately starts the negative trend. There is no attempt whatsoever to soften the blow of her dilemma, as there shouldn't be. When contemplating whether life is worth existing, Prynne concludes that it is a "hopeless task." There is a theme of desperation indicated by Hawthorne's adjectives. Choosing the words that he does, Hawthorne makes it clear that the treatment of women is an atrocity worthy of scorn.

The diction of a rhetorical question lends an undeniable sense of doom to the passage. The question Hester is pondering is, "Was existence worth accepting, even to the happiest among them?" There is an undeniable mood of negativity behind this question. She's basically asking if even the happiest woman's life isn't just a complete waste of time. Finally, after much internal debate, Hester decides that life would only be worth living if the stars happened to "align" and a few conditions came true. "As a first step, the whole system of society is to be torn down, and built up anew," she utters without much hope. Even if that occurred, the nature of women would have to be altered. These conditions reinforce the feeling of desperation.

Besides the words he chooses, the images Hawthorne creates portrays Hester as she experiences an epiphany regarding the "insurmountable precipice" facing women. The stark contrast of Prynne before and after this realization is depicted with, "Hester Prynne, whose heart had lost its regular and healthy throb." By stating in obvious terms the "throb" that her heart had before, the author makes clear that even the strongest of women were broken by the era. Mental unrest is often hard to explain, but Hawthorne accurately describes Prynne's mental turbulence as a "dark labyrinth of mind." She is thinking of so many things that it feels like she is lost in a maze of doubt. Perhaps the tone can best be described in what Prynne sees as she looks around, the "wild and ghastly scenery all around her."

It is difficult to write about the persecution of a race, or gender, or religion. Sometimes it is just too painful to put into words the degradation of an entire group of people. But, Hawthorne does just that in this specific passage from *The Scarlet Letter*. When describing the life of Hester Prynne, a headstrong woman languishing in the wrong time period, Hawthorne's words are harsh. The questions are biting. And, the message is clear. Inequality is unjust, and sugar coating it is an injustice to the many women, like Prynne, without a voice of their own.

Student B

Individuals may devote their entire lives trying to fill a glass that they see as always half empty. For those who are inhibited by a restrictive society, the effort seems hopeless. Seeing that individual beliefs can be a reflection of social values, Nathaniel Hawthorne criticizes the hypocrisies of Puritan morality in *The Scarlet Letter*. The novel reveals distinct barriers and unbending rules that generate feelings of pessimism and desperation, specifically for the young Hester Prynne as seen in this excerpt from Chapter XIII. Hawthorne's diction, tone, and rhetorical strategies expose his readers to Hester's negative state of mind.

Hawthorne's diction sets the negative and gloomy tone of this selection with such phrases as "dark question" and "hopeless task" used to define Hester as a woman whose role in Puritan society is both bleak and unbendingly defined. But, she questions the meaning of life and finds that her capabilities exceed the opportunities society offers women. The author uses rhetorical questions to involve the reader in Hester's situation. "Was existence worth accepting, even to the happiest among them?" Whether asked by Hawthorne's Hester or Shakespeare's Hamlet ("To be or not to be . . ."), such a "dark" question yields a doomsday evaluation of life. Describing Hester as ". . . without a clew in the dark labyrinth of mind . . . a home and comfort nowhere . . . ," Hawthorne employs pathos in his imagery to further expose the injustices in society and to advocate change.

It is ironic that Hester's environment deemed it correct for a woman to "keep quiet;" with the repression only furthering her desire to be heard. No doubt with this in mind, Hawthorne, uses conditional sentences to emphasize the uncertainties that a woman has as to whether or not she can ". . . assume what seems a fair and suitable position." Hester questions the very "ethereal essence" of her life—"existence worth accepting."

Fairness was not a consideration for women in Puritan society. Hester is trapped by rigid boundaries that forbid her to own property or maintain an independent life. Her extreme sorrow forces her to doubt the effectiveness of her endeavors to redraw society's boundaries. Hester illustrates the idea that it is only through continued struggle that individuals may, at some point, come to see the glass as half full and being filled as they live.

Rating the Student Essays

Student A

This writer creates a strong opening and even stronger closing paragraph. And, in between, the body paragraphs present the clear thoughts of a mature writer. This essay

- Correctly identifies Hester's outlook on life;
- Cites appropriate and strong textual references;
- Thoroughly integrates citations into the sentences and paragraphs;
- Contains a couple of long, awkwardly worded sentences;
- Uses connective tissue very well;
- Demonstrates good organization.

Student B

This student writer demonstrates quite a mature voice and writing style. Smoothly integrating citations into sentences and paragraphs throughout, this high-ranking essay has a very strong second paragraph with its reference to Shakespeare. This writer also

- Demonstrates a clear understanding of the given text and the prompt;
- Presents numerous appropriate examples of the various rhetorical devices used in the text;
- Makes effective use of transitions and echo words;
- Has few, if any, syntactical errors.

Sample AP English Language Essay Prompt 3

The following remark was made by Senator Robert Byrd during a heated debate on the floor of the U.S. Senate in 2002 regarding granting the President of the United States special powers to wage war. Drawing on your own knowledge and experience, write a carefully reasoned essay which presents your position on granting the President of the United States special powers to wage war.

"Titus Livius, one of the greatest of Roman historians, said all things will be clear and distinct to the man who does not hurry. Haste is blind and improvident. Blind and improvident, Mr. President, blind and improvident."

Rubrics for Prompt 3

A High-Ranking Essay

- Clearly indicates an understanding of Livius's statement and the demands of the prompt
- Clearly takes a position regarding Byrd's reference to the Livius quotation
- Thoroughly develops a balanced argument with specific examples and historical or personal references
- Smoothly integrates examples and references into the body of each paragraph
- Adheres to the topic with transitions and other connective tissue
- Demonstrates a mature voice, diction, and syntax
- Contains few, if any, syntactical errors

Sample Student Essays

Student A

Congress recently has had to deal with one of the most difficult decisions that a country can make—war. A distinct line was drawn between hawks and doves, while many smaller divisions were created about patriotism and the midterm elections. One senator who rose above the quagmire to state definitive beliefs was Robert Byrd. He ultimately wanted more time, more information, and more debates to deal with the issue of war. In one speech he quoted Titus Livius, specifically his remarks on haste. "All things will be clear and distinct to the man who does not hurry. Haste is blind and improvident . . . blind and improvident . . . blind and improvident." This was Byrd's obvious cry for restraint; to let time provide answers to difficult questions.

Byrd did not have to look far to find support for his belief. He could have found it in Roman history, but there are many other pieces of our culture that can support this position. "Haste makes waste" is one of the most well-known and often used expressions. Similarly, the story of the tortoise and the hare is ingrained in everyone's mind as they are growing up. Those who rush end up losing, while slow and steady wins the race. Although just a fable, it has a valuable moral. Also, simple logic would dictate that since decisions are based on knowledge, and time can allow for the acquisition of more knowledge, decisions are best made with enough time given over to thorough consideration of the issue.

The maxim that haste will harm one's decision is also illustrated in many works of literature. In William Shakespeare's Hamlet, *Prince Hamlet is faced with a very difficult decision. He sees the ghost of his dead father who instructs him to kill his uncle in vengeance for his usurpation of the throne. Hamlet could have rashly, and without thought, gone and murdered his uncle Claudius, but instead he waited. He observed and inquired; eventually, he found that his uncle did, in fact, kill his father and claim the throne. However, since he waited, he became 100% sure of his actions. Acting with haste would have resulted in endless questions. He would have wondered if he had done the right thing, or was the specter just a dream. Hamlet allowed time to clarify this situation; thus, he sees his actions as justified.*

Byrd could have also looked in a history textbook. Previous military mistakes were made with decisions made without a great deal of time for deliberation. Napoleon attacking his uncooperative ally Russia ultimately led to his defeat. If instead of attacking, he had waited to see if Russia would correct its anti-French actions, perhaps all of history would be rewritten. Similarly, The World War I may have been avoided if only the rush to avenge an assassination were delayed. If Russia were not so quick to declare war on Austria, and Germany not so quick to declare war on Russia, and France and England not so fast to declare war on Germany . . . , perhaps the needless slaughter known as The Great War would have been nothing but an attempted Serbian revolution. Millions of deaths throughout history would have been prevented, if only deliberation supplanted haste.

This is the exact statement that the senator was trying to make. By using and repeating a message from the past, Robert Byrd was emphasizing that mistakes have been made in haste before: let's not repeat them. In some circumstances, sloth might not be the deadly sin as it is so often defined.

Student B

Sun Tzu argues in his book _The Art of War_, "victorious warriors win first and then go to war, while defeated warriors rush to war first and then seek to win." Tzu's observation illustrates a piece of common knowledge easily overlooked in a time of war. On the floor of the U.S. Senate, subsequent to the September 11 attacks on the World Trade Center and the Pentagon, the matter of granting the president special powers to wage war was under heated debate. Senator Robert Byrd, a democrat from West Virginia, quoted Titus Livius, emphasizing that haste in a matter as delicate as this is "blind and improvident." One doesn't need to be fluent in Tzu's school of thought to know that "jumping the gun" (or in this case, jumping to the gun) isn't the most advantageous path to follow; American history frequently illustrates this.

President Polk's administration was chiefly, if not completely, focused on the expansion of the United States into the Texas and California territories. Intransigent and bent on war, Polk disregarded simple diplomacy with the Mexican government and positioned his troops along the Rio Grande. Inevitably, conflict erupted and the Mexican War commenced. The bulk of the American people blindly supported the war, while a few such as Ralph Waldo Emerson and John C. Calhoun, openly denounced our haste to wage war. These calls for the ending of armed conquest went unanswered. President Polk's lack of careful deliberation cost the lives of more than 10,000 people, ended favorable relations with Mexico, and ultimately brought the nation closer to civil war.

In his autobiography, Ben Franklin equates the game of chess with the need of foresight in international diplomacy. He argues that in chess, much like in life, you must evaluate your current position: What advantages do I have by moving here?; How can my enemy use my move against me?, etc. You must always think three steps ahead and not rush blindly into any situation. Most importantly, you have to be aware of and be willing to deal with the consequences of your actions.

Whether he's cognizant of it or not, our current president is playing a chess game, with global politics. He has moved his pawns around Iraq; he has moved his rooks and bishops into command positions ready to lead the attack; he has moved the U.S. queen from her safety within America to the controversial and paranoid Middle East. Constantly probing Iraq for weakness, the president doesn't realize how poorly he's protecting the one piece that must be guarded at all cost—his king, which is nothing less than the best interests of the United States. Senator Byrd indicated he realized this with his remarks made on the floor of the U.S. Senate.

Swiftness is folly. Perhaps the need to end terrorism, or the need for oil is guiding the commander-in-chief's penchant for rash action. Whatever the reasons, the United States must carefully consider what we will gain and protect if we hurry into war.

Rating the Student Essays
Student A
Although this student's reference to Shakespeare is weak, the other examples presented in support of his position are strong and clearly connected to the thesis. This writer also

- Indicates a clear understanding of the quotation and the demands of the prompt;
- Successfully implies his agreement with Senator Byrd;
- Smoothly integrates examples into the sentences and paragraphs of the essay;
- Makes good use of parallel structure in paragraph 4;
- Uses good connective tissue;
- Constructs several awkwardly worded sentences;
- Demonstrates a mature voice and writing style;
- Constructs an interesting closing paragraph.

Student B

This is a strong and mature writer, and this is demonstrated especially with the strong opening and closing paragraphs, together with interesting historical references. This student also

- Indicates his understanding of the quotation and the demands of the prompt;
- Definitely takes a position and states it clearly;
- Constructs a very good chess analogy in the penultimate paragraph;
- Effectively employs transitions and echo words;
- Has few, if any, syntactical errors.

Sample Synthesis Essay Prompt

You may encounter a different type of essay prompt on the AP English Language Exam—the synthesis essay prompt (see Chapter 4). Below is an example of what this type of prompt might look like. On the actual exam, the prompt will include the text from the sources you will need to use; here, however, we have just listed examples of sources (without the accompanying text).

(Suggested reading time—15 minutes)
(Suggested writing time—40 minutes)

Cheerleading is an integral part of interscholastic sports. We have all watched the acrobatics of cheerleaders exhorting us to support the team's efforts. There are those who maintain that cheerleading should be classified as a legitimate sport. However, in a recent court decision, a federal judge has ruled that cheerleading can no longer be a recognized sport when considering allotment of funding, scholarships, and equality of opportunity.

Carefully read the following texts, including introductory information. Using at least three of the sources, synthesize the information and include it into a well-developed essay that takes a position on whether or not cheerleading should be considered a legitimate sport by our high schools and colleges. Make certain that your argument is the central thrust of your essay and that you incorporate your sources in illustrating and supporting your claim. Avoid summarizing your sources, and clearly cite them. You may cite your sources as Source A. Source B, etc., or use the descriptions in parentheses.

Source A (Underhill Court Decision)
Source B (Goodman news report)
Source C (Reilly)
Source D (Parker Cartoon)
Source E (Chart)
Source F (AACCA Report)
Source G (Majors newspaper article)

CHAPTER 12

Practice with Sample AP English Literature Exam Essays

IN THIS CHAPTER

Summary: Apply what you've learned to sample AP English Literature prompts and essays

Key Ideas
- ✪ Pull it all together
- ✪ Consider the rubrics as guidelines
- ✪ Read and assess actual student essays

"True ease in writing comes from art, not chance, As those move easiest, who have learned to dance."
—Alexander Pope

By now we hope you're exercising up a storm! The training you've undertaken guarantees that you're not leaving your essays to chance, but applying what you've learned to write easily and artfully. What better opportunity to flex and strengthen those writing muscles than by answering an AP Literature prompt? Before you write, review the following pointers.

- Read and highlight the prompt. Thoroughly deconstruct it and determine your tasks (Chapter 5).
- Read and annotate the text(s) using our previous samples as models (Chapter 6).
- Connect the task and the texts by organizing, mapping, outlining, etc. (Chapter 6).
- Develop your thesis statement (Chapter 6).
- Strive for an introduction that will capture the reader (Chapter 7).
- Write your essay, addressing the demands of the prompt and referring specifically to the text(s).

- Cite references clearly (Chapter 8).
- Connect textual citations to the meaning of your essay (Chapter 8).
- Draw conclusions based on your information, the text, and the prompt.
- Pay attention to topic adherence.
- Use transitions, echo words, and other connectors to create unity in the essay.
- For the free response question, try for unique and original insights, as opposed to more common references.
- Validate your interpretations by anchoring and supporting the ideas with textual substantiation.
- Proofread. Pay attention to words you may have left out. Have you said what you intended to say? Add or delete information neatly (Chapter 9).

Sample AP English Literature Essay Prompt 1

Just as Catherine is introduced to Mr. Townsend in this episode from *Washington Square*, by Henry James, so, too, is the reader introduced to Catherine. In a well-written essay, discuss how James reveals Catherine's complex character. Include various techniques of characterization in your essay.

Excerpt From *Washington Square* by Henry James

Mrs. Penniman, with more buckles and bangles than ever, came, of course, to the entertainment, accompanied by her niece; the Doctor, too, had promised to look in later in the evening. There was to be a good deal of dancing, and before it had gone very far, Marian Almond came up to Catherine, in company with a tall young man. She introduced the young man as a person who had a great desire to make our heroine's acquaintance, and as a cousin of Arthur Townsend, her own intended.

Marian Almond was a pretty little person of seventeen, with a very small figure and a very big sash, to the elegance of whose manners matrimony had nothing to add. She already had all the airs of a hostess, receiving the company, shaking her fan, saying that with so many people to attend to she should have no time to dance. She made a long speech about Mr. Townsend's cousin, to whom she administered a tap with her fan before turning away to other cares. Catherine had not understood all that she said; her attention was given to enjoying Marian's ease of manner and flow of ideas, and to looking at the young man, who was remarkably handsome. She had succeeded, however, as she often failed to do when people were presented to her, in catching his name, which appeared to be the same as that of Marian's little stockbroker. Catherine was always agitated by an introduction; it seemed a difficult moment, and she wondered that some people—her new acquaintance at this moment, for instance—should mind it so little. She wondered what she ought to say, and what would be the consequences of her saying nothing. The consequences at present were very agreeable. Mr. Townsend, leaving her no time for embarrassment, began to talk with an easy smile, as if he had known her for a year.

"What a delightful party! What a charming house! What an interesting family! What a pretty girl your cousin is!"

These observations, in themselves of no great profundity, Mr. Townsend seemed to offer for what they were worth, and as a contribution to an acquaintance. He looked straight into Catherine's eyes. She answered nothing; she only listened, and looked at him; and he, as if he expected no particular reply, went on to say many other things in the same comfortable and natural manner. Catherine, though she felt tongue-tied, was conscious of no embarrassment; it seemed proper that he should talk, and that she should simply look at him. What made it natural was that he was so handsome, or rather, as she phrased it to herself, so beautiful. The music had been silent for a while, but it suddenly began again; and then he asked her, with a deeper, intenser smile, if she would do him the honour of dancing with him. Even to this inquiry she gave no audible assent; she simply let him put his arm round her waist—as she did so it occurred to her more vividly than it had ever done before, that this was a singular place for a gentleman's arm to be—and in a moment he was guiding her round the room in the harmonious rotation of the polka. When they paused she felt that she was red; and then, for some moments, she stopped looking at him. She fanned herself, and looked at the flowers that were painted on her fan. He asked her if she would begin again, and she hesitated to answer, still looking at the flowers.

"Does it make you dizzy?" he asked, in a tone of great kindness.

Then Catherine looked up at him; he was certainly beautiful, and not at all red. "Yes," she said; she hardly knew why, for dancing had never made her dizzy.

"Ah, well, in that case," said Mr. Townsend, "we will sit still and talk. I will find a good place to sit."

He found a good place—a charming place; a little sofa that seemed meant only for two persons. The rooms by this time were very full; the dancers increased in number, and people stood close in front of them, turning their backs, so that Catherine and her companion seemed secluded and unobserved. "We will talk," the young man had said; but he still did all the talking. Catherine leaned back in her place, with her eyes fixed upon him, smiling and thinking him very clever. He had features like young men in pictures; Catherine had never seen such features—so delicate, so chiseled and finished—among the young New Yorkers whom she passed in the streets and met at parties. He was tall and slim, but he looked extremely strong. Catherine thought he looked like a statue. But a statue would not talk like that, and, above all, would not have eyes of so rare a colour. He had never been at Mrs. Almond's before; he felt very much like a stranger; and it was very kind of Catherine to take pity on him. He was Arthur Townsend's cousin—not very near; several times removed—and Arthur had brought him to present him to the family. In fact, he was a great stranger in New York. It was his native place; but he had not been there for many years. He had been knocking about the world, and living in far-away lands; he had only come back a month or two before. New York was very pleasant, only he felt lonely.

"You see, people forget you," he said, smiling at Catherine with his delightful gaze, while he leaned forward obliquely, turning towards her, with his elbows on his knees.

It seemed to Catherine that no one who had once seen him would ever forget him; but though she made this reflection she kept it to herself, almost as you would keep something precious.

They sat there for some time. He was very amusing. He asked her about the people that were near them; he tried to guess who some of them were, and he made the most laughable mistakes. He criticized them very freely, in a positive, off-hand way. Catherine had never heard any one—especially any young man—talk just like that. It was the way a young man might talk in a novel; or better still, in a play, on the stage, close before the footlights, looking at the audience, and with every one looking at him, so that you wondered at his presence of mind. And yet Mr. Townsend was not like an actor; he seemed so sincere, so natural. This was very interesting; but in the midst of it Marian Almond came pushing through the crowd, with a little ironical cry, when she found these young people still together, which made every one turn round, and cost Catherine a conscious blush. Marian broke up their talk, and told Mr. Townsend—whom she treated as if she were already married, and he had become her cousin—to run away to her mother, who had been wishing for the last half-hour to introduce him to Mr. Almond.

"We shall meet again!" he said to Catherine as he left her, and Catherine thought it a very original speech.

Rubrics for Prompt 1

The following apply to a high-rated essay:

- Indicates complete understanding and support of the prompt
- Uses appropriate literary techniques to illustrate how James reveals the character of Catherine
- Thoroughly explores the methods of characterization
- Fully presents Catherine's character
- Recognizes the underlying contrasts between Marion and Catherine
- Understands the developing relationship between Catherine and Mr. Townsend
- Understands the uses of narration in the passage
- Addresses the use of dialogue with regard to character
- Recognizes tone and mood and their relation to the prompt
- Responds insightfully to image, diction, and setting
- Presents suitable interpretations of the text and subtext
- Supports the thesis with appropriate details and examples
- Integrates references smoothly
- Catches the subtleties of the passage
- Presents inferences based on the text
- Uses transitions and echo words
- Demonstrates a mature writing style
- Exhibits few, if any, syntactical errors

Sample Student Essays

Student A

In this selection from Henry James's <u>Washington Square</u>, the reader is introduced to a very shy and simple character named Catherine. Although Catherine speaks only once, replying, "yes," when asked if she felt dizzy, Henry James uses other methods to give the reader an idea about her physical appearance, personality, and emotions. These narrative devices provide a portrait of a young woman, "always agitated by an introduction."

The third person, or omniscient narration used in this passage gives the reader a picture of the party scene and the characters attending it. Although Catherine's only dialogue throughout the entire piece is, "yes," when asked if she felt dizzy, we are able to know what she is feeling and thinking. For example, when she notices how handsome or "beautiful" Mr. Townsend is, she says nothing. "Though she made this reflection, she kept it to herself, almost as you would keep something precious." We can see from this and from other examples that she is a timid girl, deficient in social skills. She has trouble initially being introduced to Mr. Townsend and anecdotal remarks from the narrator inform us that, she is "always agitated by an introduction." The narrator also reveals that Catherine is impressed by Mr. Townsend's clever remarks and smooth conversation, but she says nothing. She also finds him very amusing, but she says nothing. Even at the end of the passage, when Marian Almond tears Mr. Townsend away from Catherine, she does not even reply to his farewell, but just gazes at him. James said she is "tongue-tied" and that, "it seemed proper that he should talk, and she should simply look at him."

Catherine's observations, which are revealed by the narrator, tell us a lot about her personality. In her quietness, she is observant and has a strong aesthetic sense. She is instantaneously infatuated with Mr. Townsend because when he spoke to her, "she answered nothing; she only listened, and looked at him." She thinks he is "beautiful," rather than simply "handsome," which makes him seem god-like. This also shows her naïveté; Catherine's adulation of Mr. Townsend makes it seem as if she has never seen a man before in her life. She compares him to "young men in pictures," says he "looked like a statue," and equates his use of language with "the way a young man might talk in a novel; or better still, in a play, on the stage, close before the footlights." From Catherine's observations of Mr. Townsend, we can learn two things about her personality: first, that she can appreciate beauty around her, and second, that physical appearance can easily hoodwink her. She knows nothing about Mr. Townsend, other than from his physical appearance and from his banter, yet she feels that he is "so sincere, so natural." Catherine seems exceedingly eager to trust this "great stranger in New York," a man she barely knows anything about.

Catherine's interactions with others in the story also exemplify her simplicity and innocence, as well as her lack of self-esteem and assertiveness. She obviously does not feel good enough for a man as handsome as Mr. Townsend. "She wondered that some people—her new acquaintance at this moment, for instance—should mind it [her inability to interact or converse] so little." She is well aware of her own social anxiety in the party setting and has very low self-esteem. This is evident in her interaction with Marian Almond. She admires Marian and wonders at her social skills and confidence, "she already had all the airs of a hostess, receiving the company . . ." At the end of the story, when Marian breaks up the conversation between Mr. Townsend and Catherine, Catherine says nothing; she sits back and allows Marian to escort Mr. Townsend away. This shows that she does not know how to stand up for herself and perhaps has a fear of people who are more aggressive and more confident than she is. She feels incapable of saying anything intelligent (or anything at all for that matter), which is possibly why she does not speak and admires Mr. Townsend's "cleverness." Catherine is the type of woman whose low self-confidence would enable others to trample all over her.

Catherine's character is certainly developed by the contrast between her and the character of Marian Almond. There is also an obvious distinction between her and Mr. Townsend, as well. Marian is perhaps the type of girl Catherine would like to be, but would never have the self-confidence to become. Catherine admires her "small figure" and her "elegance." From her admiration of Mr. Townsend's "beauty," it is further intimated that Catherine may not be the most elegant or stunning woman in the room. From Catherine's extreme appreciation of the attractiveness of the other characters, the reader is given the basis to imagine that she, herself, is very plain. Catherine also admires Marian's and Mr. Townsend's cleverness. She is very impressed with the flow of words and ideas in Marian's welcoming speech: "Catherine had not understood all that she said; her attention was given to enjoying Marian's ease of manner and flow of ideas." Even Mr. Townsend's farewell, "We shall meet again!" awed Catherine. Catherine's admiration of the usage of simple conventions of language shows the reader that she was not very worldly.

Henry James allows the reader to learn about an introverted, passive, and naïve woman without directly saying so in this selection from <u>Washington Square</u>. Instead of telling the reader about Catherine, he allows us to envision her for ourselves through the use of omniscient narration, Catherine's observations, her interactions with others, and by contrasting her with other characters. Through clues and cues placed throughout the story, the reader can develop a picture of Catherine's physical appearance, her intelligence, and her personality. From James's keen characterization, the reader can deduce that Catherine is a simple woman whose ingenuousness will lead her into trouble as the rest of the story unfolds.

Student B

First impressions often leave an indelible mark on a person and future meetings often harken back to the original rendezvous. Henry James, author of <u>Washington Square</u>, understands this and emphasizes this point to the reader. It is from this point on that the reader sees Catherine's true self and the weakness that is present in her character. The reader, not only is introduced to Catherine through her statements, but also through James's structural and contextual selections. Moreover, Catherine's overall nature is exemplified by James's use of characterization, word choice, punctuation, and imagery.

Foremost, Catherine is a submissive girl who dutifully follows orders given to her, a trait characteristic of young women of that time period. This is emphasized by her dearth of communication. Mr. Townsend thoroughly dominates the conversation between Catherine and himself barely allowing her to speak, as is evidenced in the statements, "She answered nothing; she only listened" and "she felt tongue-tied." This notion of submissiveness is underscored by Catherine's usage of the sole word, "yes." There are abundant illustrations that further illustrate her compliant nature, specifically, Catherine's hesitation to answer questions: "She gave no audible assent," Mr. Townsend's speaking for both of them, "We will sit and talk.," and Mr. Townsend's control of the actions between the two "I will find a good place . . ." all serve to reinforce her submissive role.

James portrays Catherine as an inept girl who is unable to manage social situations and must rely on the help of others for guidance. The author utilizes dashes throughout the passage as a representation of the break in continuity that new introductions cause in Catherine's mind. The dashes also precede Marian Almond's interruption of Catherine's conversation which further demonstrates the interruptive power of the dash with regard to Catherine's personality.

Catherine is enamored with Mr. Townsend, yet lacks self-confidence and belief in her own capabilities. She is cognizant of her own awkwardness in social situations and introductions. Nonetheless, she praises the abilities of others, Mr. Townsend in particular, for their ability to remain calm during introductions. Thereafter, Mr. Townsend remarks "You see, people forget you." Rather than respond to his comment, Catherine muses that no individual could forget Mr. Townsend.

This section of <u>Washington Square</u> is teeming with color imagery which further establishes Catherine's character traits. The use of red, which can typify the color of a face flushed with embarrassment, solidifies the portrayal of Catherine's awkwardness. However, red is also the color of passion and love, and in the final paragraph, James writes how Catherine blushes and turns red. Finally, the image of flowers is a recurring motif. Reinforcing the color imagery, flowers are often red. Catherine is analogous to a flower for she is a soft and delicate creature. Flowers are utilized as decorations and do not necessarily add anything of substance. Likewise, Catherine is solely meant to be gazed upon and is incapable of contributing anything of importance in her conversations with Mr. Townsend.

Throughout the passage Catherine is led by Mr. Townsend, and although she fails to speak her mind or respond in her conversations with Mr. Townsend, the reader, nevertheless, gains an in-depth understanding of her disposition. Catherine's lack of self-confidence and desire to be loved is patent. Her insecurities and meek nature are readily apparent with even the most cursory of glances.

Rating the Student Essays

Student A

This high-ranking essay presents a solid, mature, and insightful discussion and analysis of Catherine's character and how James reveals it. This student writer:

- Indicates complete understanding of the prompt;
- Cites appropriate details to support the thesis:
  - Narration,
  - Contrast,
  - Character interaction;
- Has a definite, clear progression of thought and a strong writer's voice;
- Presents unique insights into the underlying theme;
- Demonstrates good topic adherence, transitions and, connective tissue;
- Uses inferences rather than plot to address the task.

Student B

This is a very effective essay because of its very unique stance and observations. This writer:

- Demonstrates a complete understanding of the prompt and the given text;
- Fully understands various methods of characterization;
- Correctly analyzes Catherine's character and how she is revealed to the reader;
- Utilizes references to support sophisticated insights;
- Responds to the subtleties of the subtext;
- Effectively analyzes Mr. Townsend and his role in the scene;
- Responds to the uses of language and punctuation in the text;
- Demonstrates mature syntax and vocabulary.

Sample AP English Literature Essay Prompt 2

The following is an excerpt from a poem entitled "Morituri Salutamus," written and presented by Henry Wadsworth Longfellow on the fiftieth anniversary of the graduation of the class of 1825 in Bowdoin College.

In a well-written essay, discuss the various perceptions of aging the poet presents and analyze the literary techniques and devices he employs to develop his ideas. Refer to such elements of the poet's craft as imagery, metaphor, contrast, and symbol.

"Morituri Salutamus" by Henry Wadsworth Longfellow

"O Cæsar, we who are about to die
Salute you!" was the gladiators' cry
In the arena, standing face to face
With death and with the Roman populace.

Young men, whose generous hearts are beating high,   5
We who are old, and are about to die,
Salute you; hail you; take your hands in ours,
And crown you with our welcome as with flowers!

How beautiful is youth! how bright it gleams
With its illusions, aspirations, dreams!   10
Book of Beginnings, Story without End,
Each maid a heroine, and each man a friend!
Aladdin's Lamp, and Fortunatus' Purse,
That holds the treasures of the universe!
All possibilities are in its hands,   15
No danger daunts it, and no foe withstands;
Hail, my companions, comrades, classmates, friends!

Ah me! the fifty years since last we met
Seem to me fifty folios bound and set
By Time, the great transcriber, on his shelves,   20
Wherein are written the histories of ourselves.
What tragedies, what comedies, are there;
What joy and grief, what rapture and despair!
What chronicles of triumph and defeat,
Of struggle, and temptation, and retreat!   25

But why, you ask me, should this tale be told
To men grown old, or who are growing old?
It is too late! Ah, nothing is too late
Till the tired heart shall cease to palpitate.
Cato learned Greek at eighty; Sophocles   30
Wrote his grand Oedipus, and Simonides
Bore off the prize of verse from his compeers,
When each had numbered more than fourscore years,
And Theophrastus, at fourscore and ten,
Had but begun his "Characters of Men."   35
Chaucer, at Woodstock with the nightingales,
At sixty wrote the Canterbury Tales;
Goethe at Weimar, toiling to the last,
Completed Faust when eighty years were past.
These are indeed exceptions; but they show   40
How far the gulf-stream of our youth may flow
Into the arctic regions of our lives,
Where little else than life itself survives.

As the barometer foretells the storm
While still the skies are clear, the weather warm   45
So something in us, as old age draws near,
Betrays the pressure of the atmosphere.
The nimble mercury, ere we are aware,
Descends the elastic ladder of the air;
The telltale blood in artery and vein   50
Sinks from its higher levels in the brain;
Whatever poet, orator, or sage
May say of it, old age is still old age.
It is the waning, not the crescent moon;
The dusk of evening, not the blaze of noon   55
It is not strength, but weakness; not desire,
But its surcease; not the fierce heat of fire,
The burning and consuming element,
But that of ashes and of embers spent,
In which some living sparks we still discern,   60
Enough to warm, but not enough to burn.

What then? Shall we sit idly down and say
The night hath come; it is no longer day?
The night hath not yet come; we are not quite
Cut off from labor by the failing light;   65
Something remains for us to do or dare;
Even the oldest tree some fruit may bear;
Not Oedipus Coloneus, or Greek Ode,
Or tales of pilgrims that one morning rode
Out of the gateway of the Tabard Inn,   70
But other something, would we but begin;
For age is opportunity no less
Than youth itself, though in another dress,
And as the evening twilight fades away
The sky is filled with stars, invisible by day.   75

Rubrics for Prompt 2

The following apply to a high-range essay:

- Indicates complete understanding of the requirements of the prompt
- Refers accurately to the thesis involving the contrast between the extremes of youth and age
- Understands the title and its appropriateness
- Recognizes and identifies the various perceptions of aging presented
- Utilizes appropriate references and details to present a coherent distinction between youth and age
- Is sensitive to the complex allusions, conceits, and diction
- Perceives Longfellow's tone and intent
- Identifies the basis of Longfellow's argument
- Identifies the poetic devices presented
- Interprets metaphors, images, symbols, etc.
- Responds to the imagery in the final stanza
- Uses smooth transitions and clear connective tissue
- Demonstrates a mature writing style

Sample Student Essays

Student A

In an address to his former classmates at the 50-year reunion of Bowdoin College's class of 1825, Henry Wadsworth Longfellow set out to invigorate and restore purpose to the lives of his elderly former classmates. Regardless of age, Longfellow asserts, human beings have the capacity for greatness. "Morituri Salutamus," takes a great philosophic leap. Old age is not a time for withering away, claims the septuagenarian poet, but a time for new explorations, new adventures, and new discoveries. Longfellow's poem itself proves great deeds can be accomplished toward the end of a lifetime. Vivid imagery, classic metaphors, relevant symbols, and deliberate structure contribute to making "Morituri Salutamus" an inspirational poem regarding a normally taboo subject—death.

The excerpt begins with a grand and powerful symbol, an allusion to the great gladiators of Rome. These courageous men stared death in the face, says Longfellow, even as their youths were in full bloom. The message is clear: If young men can face death so valiantly, the elderly can, too. In the ensuing lines, Longfellow acknowledges missing youth, utilizing images such as, "Book of Beginnings, Story without End, Aladdin's Lamp, and Fortunatus' Purse," to describe the beauty of early life. In this part of the poem words like "flowers, aspirations, dreams, and treasures" help create a light and airy mood. The simple ABABAB rhyme scheme is almost childish, harkening back to the good old days of nursery rhymes and fairy tales. The first 25 lines do not state a message, but set the stage for Longfellow's upcoming advice.

The rhetorical question, "But why you ask me, should this tale be told/ To men grown old, or who are growing old?" signals a transition in the poem. Now, Longfellow will discuss why his previous words are relevant to the group of elderly men assembled before him. Almost spontaneously, he shoots off a list of men who have accomplished great feats in the twilight of their lives. Cato, Sophocles, Simonides, Theophrastus, Chaucer, and Goethe are mentioned with their works. Longfellow's method is simple and effective; by providing concrete examples, he adds weight to his claim that old age is not a burden.

After the intensity of the previous dozen lines, Longfellow steps back and reflects upon the realities of old age. "These are indeed exceptions," he admits, "but they show/ How far the gulf-stream of our youth may flow/ Into the arctic regions of our lives." The water metaphors are certainly evocative; youth is filled with the heat and passion of the gulf-stream, while old age seems to descend into the frigidness and desolation of the arctic. Still, the arctic has a beauty all its own, and Longfellow believes this unique beauty can be tapped for creative pursuits. In almost mournful fashion, the poem continues to focus on the symbolic difference between hot and cold. Old age is the "waning, not the crescent moon/ The dusk of evening, not the blaze of noon . . . Not the fierce heat of fire/ The burning and consuming element/ But that of ashes and embers spent." The tone of this portion is dark and resigned, in stark contrast to the rest of the poem. Here, Longfellow almost seems to give up hope; the isolated successes are a farce, and the elderly should just shut themselves up to die.

The moment of decision comes in lines 62 and 63. "What then? Shall we sit idly down and say/ The night hath come; it is no longer day?" Longfellow follows this rhetorical question with a call to action. With an avalanche of metaphors and symbols, Longfellow asserts that the elderly can accomplish something. "The night hath not yet come," therefore, go out and do something! He finishes the poem with the lines, "And as the evening twilight fades away/ The sky is filled with stars, invisible by day." In essence, Longfellow says the wisdom of years can create opportunities that did not exist during youth. Finally, disappearing light creates a sense of urgency. Before long, the sky will be black forever, so expand your mind while you have the chance. Instead of fading quietly into the distance, Longfellow advises, leave the earth with a flourish of activity and determination.

Student B

The nearing of the cold winter, the falling of night, the dying fire—these have always been a poet's best metaphors for aging and death. However, in Longfellow's poem, "Morituri Salutamus," he sees in aging not the end of what used to be the peak of one's life. Instead he perceives aging as the last few opportunities for greatness that must be seized.

In the first 25 lines of his poem, Longfellow reveres the drama and glory of youth. In his youth, man can "stand face to face with death." Addressing death directly allows Longfellow to demonstrate youth's fearlessness and invincible disposition. Longfellow's constant use of exclamation points enhances the soaring, invulnerable qualities of youth. In addition, he uses words such as "illusions, aspirations, dreams," in succession, again to emphasize how incredible life can be when one is young.

Longfellow introduces a new segment of the poem with a rhetorical question. If this poem is directed toward, or, as the title suggests, written by dying people, why would Longfellow write about the splendors of youth? He explains that it is not too late for old men to be reminded of stories of young acts of heroism. It is not too late until one is officially pronounced dead. He then goes on to give examples of men in their old age that still managed to accomplish astonishing intellectual achievements. Indeed, the examples that Longfellow provides of the accomplishments of the older men are of an academic and theoretical nature, while the examples for men in their youth are mainly acts of bravery in conflict. By doing so he asserts that while the young have their strength, the elders are far nobler because they have wit and experience.

With a compassionate tone, Longfellow remarks that he understands that the men he had provided as examples were indeed exceptional. However, he uses them only to prove that humans, even in the "arctic regions" of their lives, can continue to exist and achieve great deeds.

Following his statement of honesty, Longfellow uses imagery to portray how most people perceive aging and its inevitable outcome. As he describes the "tell-tale blood" that "sinks from its higher levels in the brain," it seems as though Longfellow has given up on his optimistic view of aging. After all, he proclaims, "old age is still old age." He even uses the commonplace metaphors of a "waning moon," and the "dusk of evening."

However, the poem takes a turn yet again when Longfellow remarks that there are some "sparks left in a dead fire which can still glow." Again, Longfellow uses a rhetorical question to ask how we should respond to nature's warnings. In this final section, Longfellow reminds us that age provides every opportunity that youth does. In his final sentence he reminds us that even as dusk turns into night, the stars, our legacy, still burn at night. They remind us of what we are able to accomplish even as night begins to fall.

Rating the Student Essays

Student A

With great facility, this writer analyzes the essence of Longfellow's poem, capturing the various tones and moods of the work. This essay:

- Presents perceptive insights regarding aging and death;
- Provides strong textual support for the analytical points;
- Includes unique interpretations of imagery;
- Thoroughly analyzes the progression of ideas presented in the poem;
- Demonstrates a facility with poetic language and devices;
- Uses vivid diction with a smooth, mature writing style.

Student B

This writer effectively utilizes textual references to support his insightful analysis. The sensitivity to the contrast of youth and age raises the quality of the essay as a whole. This student is also not afraid to be critical of the poet's craft, revealing a mature sense of literary style. This student:

- Accurately addresses the prompt;
- Understands the poet's position on aging;
- Refers to suitable textual material to support the thesis;
- Demonstrates an ability to handle poetic analysis;
- Stays on topic;
- Covers the scope of the passage;
- Identifies the tone accurately;
- Draws appropriate connections and inferences;
- Uses transitions and connective tissue.

Sample AP English Literature Essay Prompt 3

A secret is a double-edged sword. It is a burden to be kept, and it is a temptation to be revealed. Each decision brings with it consequences that can affect and alter the direction and meaning of a work of literature.

From the full-length works you have studied, choose one in which a secret revealed or a secret withheld contributes to the development of theme, character, or conflict. Discuss the nature of the secret, its complexities, consequences, and the effects it has on meaning in the work.

You may choose from the following list or another full-length novel or play of literary merit.

Hamlet	*Invisible Man*
Beloved	*Twelfth Night*
The Great Gatsby	*Desire Under the Elms*
Heart of Darkness	*A Streetcar Named Desire*
Oedipus	*Frankenstein*
The Turn of the Screw	*Hedda Gabler*

Rubrics for Question 3

The following apply to a high-range essay:

- Effectively and coherently addresses the prompt
- Clearly delineates the nature of the secret and its consequences
- Chooses an appropriate novel or play
- Includes insightful references to support and illustrate the effects of the secret and their relation to meaning
- Thoroughly discusses the character's nature and its relation to the theme
- Clearly adheres to the topic
- Develops the thesis with substantial evidence
- Demonstrates a mature writing style

Sample Student Essays

Student A

"Secrets, secrets are no fun/Secrets, secrets hurt someone," goes an old childhood rhyme. Though a mere, childlike poem, it contains a good deal of truth. A secret can be as burdensome to keep as Christian's load in the novel, A Pilgrim's Progress, or as tempting to reveal as the serpent's apple in the Garden of Eden. In literature, a secret kept or a secret withheld affects the themes, characters, and conflicts within the story. Specifically, in the novel The Scarlet Letter by Nathaniel Hawthorne, the protagonists, Hester Prynne and Reverend Arthur Dimmesdale, two members of seventeenth century Puritan society, possess a secret that deeply influences the novel's themes, characters, conflicts, and symbols.

Between Hester Prynne and Reverend Dimmesdale exists a secret of a forbidden love and passion, a secret of adultery, manifested by Pearl their illegitimate child. Since their meetings often take place in the forest, the covert sin emphasizes the importance of physical settings within the novel, evoking a motif of civilization versus wilderness. Symbolically, the forest becomes a place where witches gather, souls sign themselves to the devil, and Dimmesdale can "yield himself with delicate choice . . . to what he knew was deadly sin." However, it is also a place where Hester can throw away her scarlet letter, the symbolic sign of sin, and where lovers can freely embrace; it is a place of freedom governed by natural laws, as opposed to the artificial, strict community of man-made Puritan law. The woods, a place of possibility and frankness, are in conflict with the Puritan town where order, harsh punishment, and the burden of secrecy reign.

Because Hester admits to committing adultery and Dimmesdale does not, the secret of their love and sin heavily influences the characters' developments. For Hester, who must stand on the scaffold and wear the scarlet letter "A," the secret is out in the open, lifting the burden of guilt off her shoulders. Later in the novel, the "A" on her bosom ceases being a sign of infamy and begins to stand for "able." However, for Dimmesdale the secret remains hidden, and he constantly stands with "his hand over his heart," a symbol of his "concealed sin." His continuous refusal to reveal that he is Pearl's father weighs upon his conscience, and the secret remains hidden deep within his soul, destroying his heart and body, eventually bringing about his demise, standing as a stark contrast to Hester, who has the "embroidered letter glimmering on her bosom."

Due to this secret surrounding her birth, Pearl is described as an imp, a child incapable of becoming a member of Puritan society. As a living scarlet letter, Pearl urges the Reverend to admit his secret, and only after he admits his sin is she described as a human being.

The clandestine sin creates themes and symbols in the novel. The scaffold, ironically a place of humiliation, is the one place that can grant salvation to Dimmesdale and Hester. In the second scaffold scene, Dimmesdale stands at night with Hester and Pearl, the darkness symbolizing his inner suffering and inability to publicly acknowledge the secret. The three stand "as if it were the light that is to reveal all secrets, representing the truth and freedom that the scaffold holds." It is only at the end when Dimmesdale stands on the scaffold and publicly admits to the secret that he can be freed.

Hawthorne's main message and theme in the novel is described in the epilogue as, "Be true! Be true," vehemently urging all to reveal secrets and sins. Evil is not always within the transgression but may be within the secrecy and concealment of the offense.

Student B

Unveiled to the world, a secret may have disastrous effects, yet a secret withheld could also produce dire consequences. In Mary Shelley's Frankenstein, Victor Frankenstein has a terrible secret hidden away from the world, one that has disastrous effects upon the world he is trying to protect and upon himself.

Originally intended to be a laudable achievement, Victor's secret was a life-changing mistake. He creates life, an unthinkable accomplishment that, at first, seems to have only good dividends. However, the burden of playing a god is too great for Victor, and he suffers for his actions. As a result of the responsibility and guilt of this secret, Frankenstein suffers both emotionally and physically.

Physically, Victor is distraught and wracked with illness after his monster claims the lives of family members and close friends, including his best friend Clerval. Depressed, Frankenstein has several episodes of sickness where he is too weak to get out of bed.

Emotionally, Victor suffers even more. His friend is framed for the murder of his brother, and although he knows it is his creation that is guilty, he can not bring himself to give up his secret. These resulting bouts of depression contribute to his physical ailments, also.

Although this secret affects him greatly, he is not the only one to suffer. Due to his poor choices, Victor places society-at-large in danger. But, fortunately, the monster wants revenge only on Frankenstein, not the human race in general. The monster's threat to "be with you [Frankenstein] on your wedding night" could just easily have been a threat to mankind.

Using the narrative about the creation of the monster, Mary Shelley's novel focuses on the effects that having dangerous secrets can have on the individual and society. If Frankenstein told the authorities about his monster at any point in the novel, something could have been done to ensure everyone's safety. The secrets that man keeps can change a person, a family, even a world. In Mary Shelley's novel Frankenstein, Victor's secret contributes to personal development that affects his entire world.

Rating the Student Essays

Student A

This essay conveys the essence and effects of the secrets in *The Scarlet Letter,* providing evidence from the novel with regard to effects on character, conflict, and theme. This student:

- Understands and addresses the requirements of the prompt;
- Effectively and thoroughly presents examples and references to defend the thesis;
- Indicates a strong connection between character, theme, and the secret;
- Adeptly utilizes the vocabulary of literary analysis;
- Demonstrates excellent topic adherence;
- Uses good connective tissue;
- Presents mature insights into the theme and character relationships.

Student B

Although this essay could have benefited from further development, the material that is presented indicates a successful AP student mind at work. This essay:

- Clearly demonstrates that the writer understands the relationship between task and text;
- Includes appropriate references and interpretations;
- Incorporates unifying elements such as transitions and echo words;
- Has strong topic adherence;
- Utilizes syntax expected of an AP English student.

Appendixes

APPENDIX I

Bibliography of Recommended Authors and Texts

The following is a very selected listing of authors, both past and present. Each of these writers presents ideas in original, thought-provoking, and enlightening ways. Our recommendation is that you read as many and as much of them as you can. The more you read and examine these writers and their works, the better prepared you will be for informed thinking, discussing, and writing the AP English essay. And, there is another mind-expanding benefit. You will become much more aware of the challenging and compelling world of ideas that surround you. We invite you to accept our invitation to this complex universe.

Writers don't choose their craft; they need to write in order to face the world.
—Alice Hoffman

Suggested Classical Works and Authors

Homer	*The Iliad, The Odyssey*
The Bible	"Genesis," "Exodus," "Matthew"
Sophocles	*Antigone, Oedipus Rex*
Euripides	*Medea*
Aristotle	"On the Nature of Tragedy"
Plato	"The Apology," "The Allegory of the Cave"
Swift	*Gulliver's Travels*
Voltaire	*Candide*
Molière	*Tartuffe, The Misanthrope*
Racine	*Phaedra*
Milton	"L'Allegro," "Il Penseroso," "On His Blindness," *Paradise Lost*
Pope	"An Essay on Man," "An Essay on Criticism," "The Rape of the Lock"

Suggested Realistic Works and Authors

Chaucer	*The Canterbury Tales*
Fyodor Dostoyevsky	*Crime and Punishment*
Leo Tolstoy	*Anna Karenina*
Anton Chekov	*The Cherry Orchard*
Ernest Hemingway	*The Sun Also Rises*
Henrik Ibsen	*Hedda Gabler, A Doll's House*

Suggested Romantic Works and Authors

Anonymous	*Beowulf*
Bocaccio	*The Decameron*
Cervantes	*Don Quixote*
Shakespeare	*Hamlet, King Lear, Twelfth Night*
Goethe	*Faust*
Hawthorne	*The Scarlet Letter*
Brontë	*Jane Eyre*
Hugo	*Les Miserables*

Suggested Romantic Poets

Anonymous	The Ballads—Scottish and British
Shakespeare	The Sonnets
Robert Burns	"To a Mouse," "John Anderson," "My Jo," "A Red, Red, Rose"
William Blake	"A Poison Tree," "The Sick Rose," "London," "The Chimney Sweep"
William Wordsworth	"Tintern Abbey," "My Heart Leaps Up," "London, 1802," "The World Is Too Much With Us," "I Wondered Lonely As a Cloud," "Ode on Intimations of Immortality," "Preface to the Lyrical Ballads"
Samuel Taylor Coleridge	"Kubla Khan," "The Frost at Midnight," "The Rime of the Ancient Mariner"
George Gordon, Lord Byron	"Sonnet on Chillon," "When We Two Parted," "Maid of Athens," "The Isles of Greece," "She Walks in Beauty"
Percy Bysshe Shelley	"Ode to the West Wind," "To a Skylark," "Ozymandias"
John Keats	"On First Looking Into Chapman's Homer," "Ode to a Nightingale," "Ode on a Grecian Urn," "When I Have Fears That I May Cease to Be"
Alfred, Lord Tennyson	"Ulysses"
Robert Browning	"My Last Duchess," "Pippa's Song," "Soliloquy of the Spanish Cloister"

Suggested Impressionistic Works and Authors

Henry James	*The American, Washington Square*
Joseph Conrad	*Heart of Darkness, The Secret Sharer,* "The Lagoon"
Katherine Mansfield	"Bliss"
Kate Chopin	"Story of an Hour" *The Awakening*

Suggested Naturalistic Works and Authors

James Joyce	*Dubliners*
Eugene O'Neill	*Desire Under the Elms, The Hairy Ape, The Iceman Cometh*
T. S. Eliot	"The Hollow Men," "The Love Song of J. Alfred Prufrock"
Franz Kafka	*Metamorphosis, The Trial*
Tennessee Williams	*A Streetcar Named Desire, Cat on a Hot Tin Roof*
Frank Norris	*The Octopus*
Stephen Crane	*Maggie, A Girl of the Streets*
Upton Sinclair	*The Jungle*

Recommended Poets

Matthew Arnold	Donald Hall
W. H. Auden	Galway Kinnell
Elizabeth Bishop	Maxine Kumin
Gwendolyn Brooks	Pablo Neruda
e e cummings	Sharon Olds
T. S. Eliot	Wilfred Owen
Lawrence Ferlinghetti	Linda Pastan
Robert Francis	Edna St. Vincent Millay
Jonathan Franzen	May Swenson
Robert Graves	Dylan Thomas
Seamus Haeney	

Recommended Authors

Chinua Achebe	*Things Fall Apart*
Aeschylus	*Orestia*
Margaret Atwood	*The Handmaid's Tale*
Jane Austin	*Pride and Prejudice, Sense and Sensibility*
James Baldwin	*Go Tell It on the Mountain*
Charlotte Brontë	*Jane Eyre*
Emily Brontë	*Wuthering Heights*
Albert Camus	*The Stranger*
Willa Cather	*My Antonia, One of Ours, Death Comes to the Archbishop*
Anton Chekhov	*The Cherry Orchard*

Kate Chopin	*The Awakening*
Sandra Cisneros	*The House on Mango Street*
Joseph Conrad	*Heart of Darkness, Lord Jim, The Secret Sharer*
Stephen Crane	*The Red Badge of Courage*
Don Delillo	*White Noise*
Charles Dickens	*Great Expectations, A Tale of Two Cities*
Fyodor Dostoyevsky	*Crime and Punishment*
Theodore Dreiser	*An American Tragedy, Sister Carrie*
George Eliot	*Silas Marner, Middlemarch*
Ralph Ellison	*Invisible Man*
Euripides	*Medea*
William Faulkner	*As I Lay Dying, The Sound and the Fury*
Henry Fielding	*Tom Jones*
F. Scott Fitzgerald	*The Great Gatsby*
Gustave Flaubert	*Madame Bovary*
E. M. Forster	*A Passage to India*
Thomas Hardy	*Jude the Obscure, Tess of the D'Ubervilles*
Nathaniel Hawthorne	*The Scarlet Letter*
Joseph Heller	*Catch-22*
Ernest Hemingway	*The Sun Also Rises*
Homer	*The Iliad, The Odyssey*
Khalid Hossein	*The Kite Runner*
Zora Neale Hurston	*Their Eyes Were Watching God*
Aldous Huxley	*Brave New World*
Henrik Ibsen	*A Doll's House, Ghosts, Hedda Gabler*
Kazuo Ishiguro	*The Remains of the Day*
Henry James	*The Turn of the Screw, The American*
James Joyce	*A Portrait of the Artist as a Young Man*
Franz Kafka	*Metamorphosis, The Trial*
Ken Kesey	*One Flew Over the Cuckoo's Nest*
Maxine Hong Kingston	*The Woman Warrior*
D. H. Lawrence	*Sons and Lovers*
Gabriel Garcia Márquez	*One Hundred Years of Solitude*
Herman Melville	*Moby Dick, Billy Budd*
Arthur Miller	*Death of a Salesman, The Crucible*
Toni Morrison	*Beloved, Song of Solomon*
V. S. Naipul	*A Bend in the River*
Tim O'Brien	*The Things They Carried*
Eugene O'Neill	*Desire Under the Elms, Long Day's Journey into Night*
George Orwell	*1984*
Alan Paton	*Cry, the Beloved Country*
Jean Rhys	*Wide Sargasso Sea*
Jean-Paul Sartre	*No Exit, Nausea*
William Shakespeare	*Hamlet, King Lear, Macbeth, Othello, Twelfth Night*
George Bernard Shaw	*Major Barbara, Man and Superman, Pygmalion*
Mary Shelley	*Frankenstein*
Sophocles	*Antigone, Oedipus Rex*
John Steinbeck	*The Grapes of Wrath, Of Mice and Men, Cannery Row*
Tom Stoppard	*Rosencrantz and Guildenstern Are Dead*

Jonathan Swift	*Gulliver's Travels*
Amy Tan	*The Kitchen God's Wife*
Lee Tolstoy	*Anna Karenina*
Mark Twain	*The Adventures of Huckleberry Finn*
Voltaire	*Candide*
Kurt Vonnegut	*Slaughterhouse Five*
Alice Walker	*The Color Purple*
Edith Wharton	*Ethan Frome, The House of Mirth*
Oscar Wilde	*The Importance of Being Earnest*
Thornton Wilder	*Our Town*
Tennessee Williams	*A Streetcar Named Desire, The Glass Menagerie*
Virginia Woolf	*To the Lighthouse, A Room of One's Own*
Richard Wright	*Native Son*

Personal Writing: Journals, Autobiographies, Diaries

Maya Angelou	Malcolm X
Annie Dillard	Mary McCarthy
Frederick Douglas	Greg Mortenson
Lillian Hellman	Samuel Pepys
Helen Keller	Richard Rodriguez
Martin Luther King, Jr.	May Sarton
Maxine Hong Kingston	Richard Wright

Biographies and Histories

Walter Jackson Bate	Winston Churchill
James Boswell	Shelby Foote
Thomas Carlyle	George Trevelyan
Bruce Catton	Barbara Tuchman

Journalists and Essayists

Joseph Addison	Pauline Kael
Michael Arlen	Garrison Keillor
Matthew Arnold	Philip Lopate
Francis Bacon	John McPhee
Russell Baker	N. Scott Momaday
Harold Bloom	Anna Quindlen
G. K. Chesterton	John Ruskin
Kenneth Clark	Paul Russell
Joan Didion	Marjorie Sandor
Maureen Dowd	Susan Sontag
Nora Ephron	Richard Steele

Ann Fadiman
Thomas Friedman
Ellen Goodman
Doris Kearns Goodwin
William Hazlett
John Holt

Henry David Thoreau
Calvin Trillin
Eudora Welty
E. B. White
George Will
Paul Zimmer

Political Writing and Satire

Hannah Arendt
William F. Buckley
Simone de Beauvoir
W. E. B. DuBois
Thomas Hobbes
Thomas Jefferson
John Locke
Machiavelli

John Stuart Mill
Sir Thomas More
David Sedaris
Lincoln Steffens
Jonathan Swift
Alexis de Tocqueville
T. H. White
Tom Wolfe

Naturalists, Scientists, Adventurers

Edward Abbey
Rachel Carson
Charles Darwin
Loren Eisley
Stephen Jay Gould
William Least Heat-Moon

Verlyn Klinkenborf
Barry Lopez
Peter Matthiessen
Margaret Mead
Carl Sagan

Writers Known for Their Fiction and Nonfiction

Jonathan Franzen
Charlotte Perkins Gilman
Zora Neale Hurston
Norman Mailer

George Orwell
Jane Smiley
Virginia Woolf

APPENDIX II

Glossary of Terms

Allegory   A work that functions on a symbolic level.

Alliteration   The repetition of initial consonant sounds, such as "Peter Piper picked a peck of picked peppers."

Allusion   A reference contained in a work.

Annotate   To make personal notes on a text in order to get a better understanding of the material. These notes can include questions, an argument with the author, acknowledging a good point, a clarification of an idea.

Assertion   Your thesis, the point you wish to make in your essay.

Cacophony   Harsh and discordant sounds in a line or passage in a literary work.

Character   Those who carry out the action of the plot in literature. Major, minor, static, and dynamic are types of characters.

Comic relief   The inclusion of a humorous character or scene to contrast with the tragic elements of a work, thereby intensifying the next tragic event.

Conflict   A clash between opposing forces in a literary work, such as man versus man; man versus nature; man versus God; man versus self.

Connotation   The interpretive level of a word based on its associated images rather than its literal meaning.

Deconstruct   To break something into its parts, to identify the components of a text and to decipher each of their meanings within a given context.

Denotation   The literal or dictionary meaning of a word.

Diction   The author's choice of words.

Euphony   The pleasant, mellifluous presentation of sounds in a literary work.

Exposition   Background information presented in a literary work.

Figurative language   That body of devices that enables the writer to operate on levels other than the literal one. It includes metaphor, simile, symbol, motif, hyperbole, and others.

Flashback   A device that enables a writer to refer to past thoughts, events, and episodes.

Form   The shape or structure of a literary work.

Hyperbole   Extreme exaggeration. In "My Love is Like a Red, Red Rose," Burns speaks of loving "until all the seas run dry."

Image   A verbal approximation of a sensory impression, concept or emotion.

Imagery   The total effect of related sensory images in a work of literature.

Irony   An unexpected twist or contrast between what happens and what was intended or expected to happen. It involves dialogue and situation, and can be intentional or unplanned. Dramatic irony centers around the ignorance of those involved while the audience is aware of the circumstance.

Metaphor   A direct comparison between dissimilar things. "Your eyes are stars" is an example.

Metonymy   A figure of speech in which a representative term is used for a larger idea (The pen is mightier than the sword.)

Monologue   A speech given by one character (Hamlet's "To be or not to be . . .").

Motif   The repetition or variations of an image or idea in a work that is used to develop theme or characters.

Narrator   The speaker of a literary work.

Onomatopoeia   Words that sound like the sound they represent (hiss, gurgle, bang).

Oxymoron   An image of contradictory term (bittersweet, pretty ugly, giant economy size).

Parable   A story that operates on more than one level and usually teaches a moral lesson. (*The Pearl* by John Steinbeck is a fine example. See Allegory.)

Parody   A comic imitation of a work that ridicules the original.

Pathos   The aspects of a literary work that elicit pity from the audience.

Personification   The assigning of human qualities to inanimate objects or concepts (Wordsworth personifies "the sea that bares her bosom to the moon" in the poem "London 1802.")

Plot   A sequence of events in a literary work.

Point of view   The method of narration in a work.

Rhetorical question   One that does not expect an explicit answer. It is used to pose an idea to be considered by the speaker or audience. (Ernest Dowson asks, "Where are they now the days of wine and roses?")

Satire   A mode of writing based on ridicule, which criticizes the foibles and follies of society without necessarily offering a solution (Jonathan Swift's *Gulliver's Travels* is a great satire, which exposes mankind's condition.)

Setting   The time and place of a literary work.

Simile   An indirect comparison that uses the words *like* or *as* to link the differing items in the comparison. ("Your eyes are like stars.")

Stage directions   The specific instructions a playwright includes concerning sets, characterization, delivery, etc. (See *Hedda Gabler* by Ibsen.)

Stanza   A unit of a poem, similar in rhyme, meter, and length to other units in the poem.

Structure   The organization and form of a work.

Style   The unique way an author presents his ideas. Diction, syntax, imagery, structure, and content all contribute to a particular style.

Symbol   Something in a literary work that stands for something else. (Plato has the light of the sun symbolize truth in "The Allegory of the Cave.")

Synecdoche   A figure of speech that utilizes a part as representative of the whole. ("All hands on deck" is an example.)

Syntax   The grammatical structure of prose and poetry.

Synthesis   The integration of a number of sources into the development and support of the writer's thesis.

Theme   The underlying ideas the author illustrates through characterization, motifs, language, plot, etc.

Tone   The author's attitude toward his or her subject.

Understatement   The opposite of exaggeration. It is a technique for developing irony and/or humor where one writes or says less than intended.

Voice   The author's distinct, unique, recognizable style. Voice can also refer to *active* or *passive* when referring to whether the subject of the sentence is doing the acting or is being acted upon.

Web Sites Related to AP English

There are literally thousands of sites on the Web that are in some way related to the study of college-level English. We are not attempting to give you a comprehensive list of all of these sites. But, we are going to provide you with a list that is relevant to your preparation and review for constructing an AP English essay. It is up to you go to the sites to see for yourself just what it can offer and whether or not it will be of specific benefit to you. Each of these Web sites can lead you to many more. Perhaps, you might even decide to set up your own AP English Web site or chat room!

Note: These sites were up and running at the time this book was published. If you find a site is no longer available, we would appreciate your letting us know. We would also love to hear from you if you have found a site that you believe other students of AP English could utilize.

Since this is an Advanced Placement exam which you are preparing for, why not go to the organization that is the source of the exam as your first choice?

- http://www.collegeboard.org/ap
- http:www.collegeboard.org/ap/english

For AP exam links:

- http://maxpages.com/aptest

For an interesting AP test club and chat room:

- http://clubs.yahoo.com/clubs/aptest?s

For practice with essay questions:

- http://cbweb6.collegeboard.org/writewellCB/student/ap/html/apintro.html

A Web site focused on preparation for AP English Literature:

- http://www.kn.att.com/wired/fil/pages/listaplitma.html

A Web site focused on preparation for AP English Language:

- http://www.kn.att.com/wired/fil/pages/listaplanguma.html

Two sites useful for grammar help:

- Purdue University: http://owl.english.purdue.edu/owl/
- Grammar Bytes (terms, exercises, tips, rules from a primate with attitude!): http://chompchomp.com/menu.htm

For rhetorical and literary terms:
- http://www.uky.edu/AS/Classics/rhetoric.html
- http://andromeda.rutgers.edu/~jlynch/Terms/index.html
- http://humanities.byu.edu/rhetoric/Silva.htm

To find thousands of free e-books in over 50 languages that can be downloaded go to:

- www.bartleby.com

Also try E-Books Directory, an online resource containing links to free downloadable e-books, technical papers, and documents, as well as user-contributed content, articles, reviews, and comments:

- http://www.e-booksdirectory. com

Some claim this is the ultimate Shakespeare site

- www.PlayShakespeare.com

You can view today's front pages and compare coverage of major events in newspapers around the world:

- http://www.newseum.org/todaysfrontpages/

For access to the world of arts and letters, the following Web site offers access to newspapers, literary magazines, columnists, blogs, etc.:

- http://artsandlettersdaily.com

Web notes, a highlighting and "sticky note" tool that allows users to compile information from multiple web pages and then organize and share their findings:

- http://www.webnotes.net

Answers for Practice Activities

Chapter 3

Warm-Up 3

The answers (in order) are: Description, exposition/description, argument, narration, argument, description, narration, argument, exposition, description

Chapter 5

Self-Test (following Warm-up 17)

1. metonymy, metaphor, personification
2. simile
3. parallelism
4. allusion (the film, *Gone with the Wind*)
5. parallelism, antithesis
6. onomatopoeia, apostrophe
7. metaphor, personification, hyperbole
8. onomatopoeia, apostrophe, metaphor, personification
9. metonymy
10. onomatopoeia, alliteration
11. metaphor, personification, synecdoche
12. rhetorical question, litotes
13. understatement
14. epithet, simile
15. metaphor, epithet
16. alliteration
17. metaphor, alliteration
18. hyperbole
19. parallelism
20. oxymoron

Warm-up 18

Compound sentence: After a long flight, the pilot landed the plane at O'Hare airport, and the passengers were quite happy for the safe and smooth landing.

Complex sentence: After a long trip, the passengers were quite happy that the pilot landed the plane safely and smoothly at O'Hare Airport.

Compound–complex sentence: The pilot landed the plane at O'Hare airport, and after a long trip, the passengers were quite happy that the landing was a safe and smooth one.

Periodic sentence: After a long trip, and after a safe and smooth landing by the pilot at O'Hare Airport, the passengers were quite happy.

Warm-up 19

There are five sentences.

Sentences 1 and 4 begin with prepositional phrases.

Sentence 3 begins with a participial phrase.

Sentences 2 and 5 begin with the subject.

The two compound sentences are 2 and 5.

Sentences 1 and 4 are simple.

Sentence 3 is the only complex sentence.

The excerpt's subject is the Kaatskill Mountains.

The purpose is to describe.

The sentences do contain many descriptive phrases set off by commas.

The mountains and the Hudson River are the two items given the most coverage.

Personification is found in sentence 5.

The diction can be described as poetic, complex, graceful, and artful.

The overall effect of the passage is lyrical.

Warm-up 20

Tone is informal.

Words that characterize the tone of the review: critical and sarcastic.

Words/phrases that help develop the tone: *perfunctory, harrowing and confusing, toyed with, not acted, problem, lurid teasers, light on character development, frightens away.*

Total Workout (at the end of Chapter 5)

1. A man tells the reader his plans for killing an old man.
2. To entertain
3. 1st
4. Dash and exclamation point
5. Make parentheticals stand out and for explanatory information
6. Strong emotions
7. "Gentle" and followed by an indication of strong or sudden emotion do not go together; they in opposition
8. To go from cautiously moving to a hearing situation is unexpected and not grammatically connected to the rest of the sentence.
9. Sight and sound
10. Metaphor, rhetorical question, analogy, parallelism, onomatopoeia, litote, personification
11. Yes
12. Yes
13. Varied
14. Does not

15. *Mad, you, madman, cautiously, very, eye, old man*
16. Ironic, complex, conversational
17. Chilling, suspenseful
18. Hyperbolic, dramatic, compelling, complex
19. The second and third choices would be correct.

Chapter 6

Workout 2, Prompt A
1. A passage from the introduction to Martin Luther King's *Why We Can't Wait.*
2. Describes, analyzes
3. Rhetorical purpose of the passage, the stylistic, narrative, and persuasive devices
4. Social conditions and attitudes of black Americans in the 1960s
5. Rhetorical purpose
6. Describes and analyzes
7. Stylistic, narrative and persuasive devices
8. No

Workout 2, Prompt B
1. Two poems
2. Discuss
3. Similarities, differences
4. Contrast/comparison
5. Allusion
6. No

———